FEEDING THE HUNGRY SOUL

Spiritual Preparation for Restoration Therapy

Dr. David Johnny Nixon

Copyright© 2018 by David Johnny Nixon

Feeding the Hungry Soul:
Spiritual Preparation for Restoration Therapy
by Dr. David Johnny Nixon

Edited by: Joshua Agan and Glenn Hamm

Printed in the United States of America

ISBN: 978-1-942559-07-8

All rights reserved solely by the author. The author guarantees all content is original and does not infringe upon the legal rights of any other person or work. No part of this book may be reproduced in any form, without permission in writing from the author or publisher.

All Scripture quotations, unless otherwise indicated, are taken from the Holy Scriptures, *King James Version*.

Cover design by Joshua Agan.

Restoration Counseling Ministries

250 Doc Darbyshire Road,
PMB 210
Moultrie, GA 31788

https://restoration.care/

Dedication

To my wife Chrissy: for her love, prayer, and support. I love you.

To my parents: David and Mary Nixon, for always being true examples of compassion. Thank you!

And to my children—Kathleen, Kirsten, Kahlen, John-Boy, and Katie Grace: I love being your daddy!

Acknowledgements

I would like to thank Steve and Sarah Case for their friendship, love for people, loyalty to truth, and dedication to the ministry of restoration.

I would like to thank Glenn Hamm, my father-in-law, for his love, support, and work in the development of this material.

Thank you to those who have helped me understand the ministry of restoration: David Baker, David Hyles, S.M. Davis, Bob Gray, Rick Carter, Mark Agan, Dominic Pennachietti, Michael Nixon, Nick Nixon, Gadston and Pellie Moore, Nick Vaughn, and Jerry and Jennifer Henson.

Thank you to Pastor Chet Cooper and my church family at Crossroad Bible Church—I love you all.

A big thank you to Joshua Agan for your help in compiling this material. Without your help, this book would not have been completed.

Table of Contents

foreword By Dr. James Wilkins ix
Preface xi
1. Counseling God's Way 1
2. Beware Of Hunger 13
3. To Do Or Not To Do 29
4. Absence Demands Attention 39
5. The "Moral" Majority 47
6. The Pursuit Of Happiness 57
7. Avoiding Hunger 67
8. Fasting Away Hunger 79
9. The Fruit of the Spirit 87
10. Feasting Away Fear 103
11. Feasting For Today 111
12. Feasting On Forgiveness 117
13. Feasting For Strength 127
14. Feasting With Your Soulmate 133
15. There Is Room 141
16. God Loves Restoration 151
17. The Fullness Of God 159
18. Feed My Lambs 171
Appendix 179
About The Author 189

Foreword
by Dr. James Wilkins

I have been a full time Pastor and Evangelist for 66 years. I have worked in some of the finest colleges of our day and authored 79 books with over 2 million in circulation. Jesus Christ, our Lord, was known as a friend of sinners. He challenged the norm of His day to have compassion on those who appeared hopeless.

I find this same spirit of love and compassion in Dr. Johnny Nixon and his counseling ministry. God is using Dr. Nixon's ministry to transform the lives of thousands into useful children of God. His life has been uniquely gifted and given to the world as a conduit of godly counsel and discipleship. With wisdom beyond his years, he has become a counselor's counselor of sorts.

I am greatly appreciative of his ministry and wholeheartedly recommend him and his work.

— **Dr. James Wilkins**,
New Testament Ministries International

Preface:

THE PURPOSE OF THIS BOOK

We all do it! You do it and so do I. In fact, there is probably not a day goes by that we don't give someone advice. Sometimes it is intentional and other times it may be unintentional. Nevertheless, we often tell other people what to do.

Everybody has opinions and some people like to share their opinion more than others, even if nobody asks for it. Sometimes we are asked for our opinion and when that happens we should be careful with our response. Our advice could have a life altering impact on another person's life.

The dictionary defines advice as an opinion or recommendation offered to guide an action or conduct. The Bible uses the term counsel instead of advice. Counsel and advice are synonyms. You may think the term counsel has a deeper meaning than just giving someone advice, but the basic meaning is the same. For the purpose of this book, I will use the Biblical term ***counsel***.

Now, you may give someone counsel about something trivial like a great place to go fishing, or you may give someone life altering counsel about how to save their life or marriage. The importance and consequence of the counsel you provide will vary with each situation.

Good communication is critical, if we are going to be successful in providing good counsel. Think about it this way...do you have a favorite song? Why is it your favorite song? I don't believe you would answer, "I love this song because of its prolific polyrhythms offset with arpeggiated succession of relative minors." No, you would probably explore your feelings, emotions, and relationships associated with the song. It connects you to something or someone in some way.

When we provide counsel, we must always remember that people are not textbooks. We must avoid intellectual jargon. Instead, we must communicate in terms that can be easily understood. We should help the person find out what is distorting their life's music. Why are their feelings, emotions, and relationships disconnected? We must help them connect with and joyfully sing the new song God has placed in their heart.

Every follower of Christ wants to give good, solid counsel. No one wants to intentionally lead someone wrongly. If you are like me, at some point in your life you knew everything there was to know about everything. And then, by the Grace of God, you discovered you don't know everything. You may have realized, like me, that you need God to lead you and guide you in every decision of life. Just as important, you realized that you need God's wisdom so that you can give other people wise counsel.

Your life is guaranteed to have an impact on others, therefore you need to get it right. You need to be prepared to provide wise counsel.

CHAPTER 1

COUNSELING GOD'S WAY

There is a really good chance that you have crossed someone's path recently that was hurting deeply. They may have smiled at you and spoke kind words to you, but inside their soul was struggling with a deep, dark emptiness. We often do not realize when we meet these people with an outward appearance of happiness, yet the pain in their heart is so intense, they are entertaining thoughts of suicide. I have witnessed this many times.

It has been my privilege to counsel with a diverse group of people to include war veterans, A-list celebrities, Police Officers, Firefighters, homeless, business leaders, Olympic athletes, and professors of top universities. I have counseled those who have taken life and given life, those who have undergone terminal illness and won, and those who have undergone terminal illness and eventually lost. I have counseled the popular, the unwanted, and the outcast. I have sat down with the rich and with the homeless. I've prayed and counseled with some believers who are well known, loved, and dearly respected, and others who have fallen in life and practically been discarded.

One of the most valuable lessons that I have learned from my experience, is that we can never assume that hurting people *look* hurt. That is simply not the case. Most hurting people have become good actors and actresses. They have learned how to play the role of a happy neighbor, cheerful coworker, or successful friend, but it's really just an act. Deep inside they are dying and do not know what to do.

BEARING THE BURDEN

I do not believe that people who commit suicide want to die; they just want the pain to stop. Too often, their pain or fear is louder than rational thought. We have all been there to some degree. Have you ever experienced a pain so immediate and so intense that you are unable to think rationally, but instead you react?

I regret deeply how many people I have encountered that really needed my help, but I was too absorbed in my own problems and I did not give them the time and attention they desperately needed. God forgive me for being so selfish.

One pastor put it this way: "We should be good to everybody because everybody's having a tough time." I agree, at least we should behave like that's the case. We cannot ignore the fact that we live in a chaotic world where a continuous news cycle shows death and devastation around the globe. Stress is prevalent in every age group today like never before. Truthfully, we have no idea what one act of kindness can do to change the course of a person's life, maybe even save it. We are to bear each other's burdens and so fulfill the law of Christ.

THE MINISTRY OF RECONCILIATION

What can we do to help those people who *look normal*, but who are hurting so deeply? We should be available and usable for ministry.

Don't miss this...it is rare that you will make a real difference by accident. Effective ministry is intentional not accidental. *Mankind continues to look for **methods** while God is simply looking for men and women who are **available and usable**.* You must be prepared for service. You don't have to beg God to use you. He *will* use you if you are usable. We should make ourselves *available* and our prayer should always be for Him to make us *usable*.

That's what this book is all about. We need more believers who are usable for Christ's service. You have to make yourself available, but this book can help make you usable.

The reason more churches are not involved in restoration is because there are too few churches that promote true spirituality. The pews are filled with saved people, but not spiritual people. They are filled with people who are doing religious things by the works of the flesh rather than by walking in the Spirit. As a result, very little restoration is being carried out by them. This should not be so. It is my firm belief that every believer is a counselor in one way or another. The question is, what type of counsel are they providing?

The Holy Spirit is essential when it comes to the work of one who seeks to counsel scripturally. The Holy Spirit is called the Counselor, Comforter, Helper, and Advocate in God's Word (John 14:16–17). This book is a study of spiritual fullness and the ministry of reconciliation.

TRUE SATISFACTION

We are all searching for something. There is a hunger within the human heart, an aching sense of something unfinished or undone. It is a feeling that plagues us. The hunger is relentless, always seeking the infinite, desiring to find something larger than ourselves.

These feelings are a sacred warning. The emptiness is a hollow reminder that we need to seek God for fulfillment. When we try to satisfy the emptiness with substitutes for God -- objects, money, love, pleasure, sex, drugs, new experiences, or whatever is at hand, our lives will be filled with feelings of unrest and dissatisfaction:

If only they would hire me...
If only we could move...
If only she'd go out with me...
If only I could make the football team...
If only I could have her looks...

If only I had more money…

When you're trying to change your life, or create specific results, you need to understand the cause and effect of your actions. Understanding the cause is necessary—true satisfaction means yielding spiritual control of your life to God.

NOT GOD'S WAY

When a person doesn't know what's wrong and their life feels out of control, the world around them will seem unpredictable and chaotic. Sometimes, the same behavior or methods appear to produce varying results. All their hard work may appear useless. In moments like those, it may seem like the world has ended--it hasn't!

How does a Christian handle the seemingly overwhelming problems of this life?

The world has its own system of values and philosophy for coping with problems. But, are these values and philosophies consistent with the teachings of the Bible? Are they truly valuable and helpful? Or, do they represent a system of ideas and methods that are in direct conflict with Scripture?

We must not be deceived. To begin a closer examination of how God's Word clashes with secular psychology, we must establish a basic framework for discussion. The Words of God in Isaiah are a good place to begin. "*'Woe to the rebellious children,' saith the Lord, that take counsel, but not of Me*" (Isaiah 30:1) God has clearly told us that our counsel must be rooted in Him alone.

COUNSELING GOD'S WAY

> [1] Woe to them that go down to Egypt for help;
> and stay on horses, and trust in chariots,
> because they are many; and in horsemen,
> because they are very strong;
> but they look not unto the Holy One of Israel,
> neither seek the Lord!
>
> [2] Yet he also is wise, and will bring evil,
> and will not call back his words:
> but will arise against the house of the evildoers,
> and against the help of them that work iniquity.
>
> [3] Now the Egyptians are men, and not God;
> and their horses flesh, and not spirit.
> When the Lord shall stretch out his hand,
> both he that helpeth shall fall,
> and he that is holpen shall fall down,
> and they all shall fail together.
> **Isaiah 31:1-3**

Counsel apart from the Lord is not wise. In fact, it is dangerous.

What is counsel, simply stated, it is any direction that we receive through our eyes or ears.

One of my favorite portions of Scripture is found in Psalms:

> [1] Blessed is the man that walketh not
> in the counsel of the ungodly,
> nor standeth in the way of sinners,
> nor sitteth in the seat of the scornful.
>
> [2] But his delight is in the law of the LORD;
> and in his law doth he meditate day and night.
>
> [3] And he shall be like a tree planted by the rivers of water,
> that bringeth forth his fruit in his season;
> his leaf also shall not wither;
> and whatsoever he doeth shall prosper.

> [4] The ungodly are not so:
> but are like the chaff which the wind driveth away.
>
> [5] Therefore, the ungodly shall not stand in the judgment,
> nor sinners in the congregation of the righteous.
>
> [6] For the LORD knoweth the way of the righteous:
> but the way of the ungodly shall perish.
> **Psalm 1**

The term ***ungodly*** in verse 1 simply means ***not God's way.***

Are we guilty of seeking direction that inherently is not God's way?

Some people believe that psychology is a blessing if properly integrated with the Bible. After all, you might ask, couldn't there be some areas of life that are not addressed by Scripture? Is it possible that we might gain valuable insight through the addition of man-made philosophies and secular wisdom? God's Word states: "Every word of God is pure: he is a shield unto them that put their trust in Him. Add thou not unto his words, lest he reprove thee, and thou be found a liar." (Proverbs 30:5, 6)

A SECULAR PRIEST

For starters, there is a significant difference between that which is ***non-biblical*** and that which is ***anti-biblical.***

The Bible does not instruct us about how to build a light bulb or change a light bulb. We can refer to a secular textbook for that information. Why should counseling be any different?

The Bible does not mention the light bulb, but it does teach us that light is good. The light bulb may be classified as non-biblical, but it is not anti-biblical. On the other hand, the Scriptures warn us about vain philosophies that are anti-biblical.

Consider some of these questions:
- *What is the nature of man?*
- *What is man's fundamental problem?*
- *How do we relate to our fellow human beings?*
- *What values guide our attitudes and actions?*
- *How can man prosper emotionally?*
- *What are man's goals in life?*
- *Is there real hope?*

Secular psychology attempts to solve all these conundrums. That's a really big problem since the answers can **ONLY** be found **in God's Word.** It is obvious that psychology is in direct competition with God. Every system of psychological theory addresses issues that are already fully addressed in Scripture.

These psychology experts, professing to be wise, try to tell us how to handle anger, when to forgive, how to handle our relationships, how to raise children, and how to resolve every other life issue. The bible gives us the answer to all of these questions. Where there appears to be truth in psychology, time spent in biblical research will reveal that we already have **ALL** truth, in the purest form, in God's Word.

Psychology's focus is on the "***I.***" I deserve more money. I deserve more attention. I deserve to be happy. I will find myself. I will forgive myself. I will please myself.

As a result, self becomes god.

> For men shall be lovers of their own selves,
> covetous, boasters, proud, blasphemers,
> disobedient to parents, unthankful, unholy
> **2 Timothy 3:2**

FEEDING THE HUNGRY SOUL

> The wicked, through the pride of his countenance,
> will not seek after God:
> God is not in all his thoughts.
> **Psalm 10:4**

It is through biblical truth, Christ and the work of the Holy Spirit that we are justified, forgiven, cleansed of our unrighteousness, and sanctified. However, Psychiatrists inform us that we are sick people in need of psychotherapy and medicinal drugs.

When the focus is on self, the focus soon becomes a focus on feelings. Some of today's popular therapies encourage us to **get in touch with our feelings** or to **visit the past.** This is unhealthy.

Feelings become god, which in reality is another idol of the heart. In contrast, the Bible instructs us to focus on the Lord, to walk in the Spirit, and to follow His commandments. God says we are to walk by faith and not by sight.

Satan is a master manipulator of *feelings.* You don't have to be lonely to feel lonely. You might be loved by many and yet feel unloved. Feelings are not to be trusted.

Remember Isaac? When he was old and blind, he did not recognize which son stood before him. The voice sounded like Jacob, but the arms felt like Esau's. The voice was the voice of Jacob, but the hands were the hands of Esau. This had to be confusing! Isaac was fooled. He trusted his feelings.

The modern psychiatrist is a **secular priest**.

When the pastor doesn't know how to counsel a particular person, he might hurriedly refer him to the *high priests* of psychiatry. It ought to be the other way around.

A WORK IN PROGRESS

As a mentor to counselors and those who disciple, I am always growing and learning. My process is far from perfect and it continues to challenge almost every method that I have learned in the past. Some days, during counseling, I feel like I am building a plane while it is in flight. Today a wing is added, next week the tail, tomorrow the engine! So I hope in the years ahead to continue to refine this material to make it much better and more helpful.

This is not a *how to* manual for counseling. Rather, it is more like a spiritual cookbook. I pray that you will read all of it and immediately begin feasting like never before. Feasting on the fruit of the Holy Spirit—and feeding hungry souls.

FEEDING THE HUNGRY SOUL

CHAPTER 2

BEWARE OF HUNGER

FEEDING THE HUNGRY SOUL

BEWARE OF HUNGER

"What you don't know won't hurt you.
*It is that which you do **not know***
*that you **don't know***
which will hurt you."

If you are like most people, you may have to read that a few times to catch what it means. I do not know *how* to fly an airplane, and it does *not* hurt me not to know this. *Because* I know that I do not know how, I choose not to attempt it, and I remain safe on the ground.

But what if I did not *realize* that I did not know how to fly a plane? What if I thought that flying a plane was no different than driving a car? If I did not know that I didn't know how, then I might overconfidently enter a cockpit and potentially lose my life.

Herein lies one of the greatest dangers to God's people. In Hosea 4:6, God says, "My people are destroyed for their lack of knowledge." It is not an abundance of immorality that destroys His people. It is not an abundance of perversion that destroys His people. It is not the presence of any one thing that destroys them. Rather, it is the **absence** of something—*a void*—that destroys His people. Again, "My people are destroyed for their **lack of knowledge**."

I have heard a few messages in my lifetime about voids; but for the most part, they have been much too presumptive. Have you ever heard someone preach for or against something that is not in the Scriptures? That is what God calls **presumptuous** sin. They presume to speak for or against something that God does not speak for or against. *We have to be careful not to be presumptuous with God's Word.* Look up the word **presumption** in the Scriptures and you quickly find that it brings reproach upon the Lord (Numbers 15:30), and He calls for the death of any man who presumes to act or even speak where He (God) has not spoken. (Deuteronomy 17:12; 18:22).

> But the soul that doeth ought presumptuously,
> whether he be born in the land, or a stranger,
> the same reproacheth the LORD;
> and that soul shall be cut off
> from among his people.
> **Numbers 15:30**

> And the man that will do presumptuously,
> and will not hearken unto the priest
> that standeth to minister there before the LORD thy God,
> or unto the judge, even that man shall die:
> and thou shalt put away the evil from Israel.
> **Deuteronomy 17:12**

> When a prophet speaketh in the name of the LORD,
> if the thing follow not, nor come to pass,
> that is the thing which the LORD hath not spoken,
> but the prophet hath spoken it presumptuously:
> thou shalt not be afraid of him.
> **Deuteronomy 18:22**

So how can we avoid the sin of being presumptuous? We avoid it by never forsaking the perimeter of Scriptural ***precepts*** and ***principles*** found in God's Word.

PRECEPTS, PRINCIPLES, AND PRESUMPTIONS

A scriptural ***precept*** is an authoritative command. There is no confusion with a precept; it says *do* or *do not*.

Be ye holy is a precept.

Thou shalt not lie is a precept.

A scriptural *principle* is a truth drawn from generalization instead of specific commands. Principles can vary from person to person.

For example, we see Jesus pair up the disciples two by two when sending them out to minister. For safety and accountability, that is a great principle to follow, but it is *not* a precept. Some may choose to follow it and some may not.

A *presumption* is when a person presumes to do or say something on God's behalf, but God did not tell them to do or say it. This most often happens when someone preaches a personal principle as a scriptural precept.

> For precept **must be** upon precept, precept upon precept; line upon line, line upon line; here a little, and there a little.
> **Isaiah 28:10**

Scriptural teaching is based on precepts, followed by the principles which support them. Biblical principles always reinforce scriptural precepts.

Understanding these terms is important for several reasons. Not only does it mean the difference between someone preaching "Thus Saith the Lord" and another preaching presumptuous heresy, which brings a reproach upon the Lord; but it can also help people recognize and escape legalistic and lascivious bondage.

A scriptural principle will always follow a scriptural precept. To understand this, it is like seeing a stop sign with a smaller sign below it that says, "*Drive Carefully.*" The word *STOP* is a precept; you must comply under penalty of law. The words *Drive Carefully* are merely a guiding principle for how you should drive for optimal safety. Part of driving carefully is to obey the stop sign.

FEEDING THE HUNGRY SOUL

When we see that Jesus paired up the disciples, it is a great principle to follow, but there is no precept that commands it. Preaching that we *must* go out two by two is presumptuous. This would be as ridiculous as seeing that Jesus and the disciples all wore sandals and then preaching that *true believers* must wear only sandals.

Every single cult on planet earth has always preached principles *as* precepts. They all are guilty of presumption; however, believers are not immune to this same danger.

One example of this is *gambling*. We find many precepts that teach us not to pursue riches. This can lead us to draw a wise principle that we should avoid gambling which is a game of chance. However, there is no precept which says *Thou shalt not leave things to chance*. In fact, even the disciples cast lots in Scripture. If someone were to preach that God condemns any game of chance that would be a presumption, not a precept.

Certainly, God's Word gives us guidelines to avoid quick riches and the pursuit of riches, but there is no precept against the game of chance. To avoid gambling, so as to be good stewards of God's resources, is a great principle that we should strive to follow. However, we cannot preach it as **Thus Saith the Lord** without being presumptuous. We should preach and teach the precept, and then appropriately attach wise principles to it.

> Let your conversation be without covetousness;
> and be content with such things as ye have.
> **Hebrews 13:5**

This is a precept. God commands us to be content; therefore, *avoiding gambling* is a good principle to follow.

*(Please note: some preachers, teachers, or counselors may often use the term **principle** in their vocabulary when in fact they mean a*

precept. We simply seek to define, explain, and exhort concerning the difference.)

Understanding these differences is also important because it helps us discern sound doctrine from garbage. Sound doctrine is important because what we *believe* affects what we *do*. Behavior is an extension of theology and there is a direct correlation between what we think and how we act.

There is probably no better example of this than the fall of Adam. He was given a precept, *freely eat,* and he failed to obey. This opened him up to Lucifer's presumptions, "God did not mean you will actually die. He knows that you will be as gods, and He just wants to withhold that from you."

Lucifer presumed to say what God did not say. Giving ear to that presumption led Adam and Eve to their spiritual deaths.

THE FALL OF MAN

It is impossible for us to fully comprehend the goodness of Adam and Eve's life in the Garden of Eden. As we read the description of all that God created, we cannot grasp the magnificence of how beautiful and perfect it was. When God made mankind, He placed them in a world filled with beauty and pleasure.

Life was really good! Think about it, Adam and Eve enjoying perfection with God. No pain, no fear, no shame, no hatred, and no regrets. Peace and harmony with each other, and most importantly, peace with God. It was perfect!

God basically commanded Adam to enjoy himself freely. *"This is yours, Adam. Enjoy every creation fully and freely."* What a life.

God placed only one stipulation on Adam.

He warned him that one tree was forbidden. There was only one fruit that he should not indulge in, but he was *commanded* to eat freely of every other tree. Adam was basically commanded to live a life of complete joy and satisfaction. Life could not have been more perfect, but what made it perfect? A pure and undefiled relationship with God made it perfect. Everything else was a glorious by-product of their perfect relationship with God.

So what could possibly cause Adam to risk losing all that he was freely given for the one thing that was forbidden?

The answer is **HUNGER.** We have all experienced hunger at some point in our lives. Hunger is an emptiness and void within. *Voids* can occur when a loved one dies, when people go through a divorce, when we experience financial problems, or any other event in life that creates emptiness. The *voids in life can easily control us* if we are not careful. How we satisfy our hunger and how we fill a void is of utmost importance.

There was a void in Adam's body (his stomach to be exact) and he was not filled.

He had no reason to be hungry. God had provided plenty for him to eat and commanded him to eat it. He had no excuse, so how did Adam satisfy his hunger? He chose to satisfy himself with the opportunity offered by Satan instead of what God had freely provided.

THE PICTURE OF CHILDBIRTH

Nothing is in Scripture by accident. God often gives seemingly peculiar instructions or statements at times, but He does so to paint a picture that teaches a larger truth. For example, God once instructed Moses to hit a rock in the middle of the wilderness in order to provide water for millions of people. This presumably absurd and impossible method of obtaining water had a purpose. God sought to paint a picture of His Son who would one day be smitten for us, providing Living Water to thirsty souls (1 Corinthians 10:4). When Moses later marred that picture, it cost him entry into the Promised Land with his people.

It is said that a picture is worth a thousand words, but I contend that every word of God is worth a thousand pictures, and He takes His pictures seriously.

Have you ever noticed the specifics of the curse? God radically altered childbirth when He passed judgment on Adam and Eve.

> Unto the woman he said,
> I will greatly multiply thy sorrow and thy conception;
> in sorrow thou shalt bring forth children;
> and thy desire shall be to thy husband,
> and he shall rule over thee."
> **Genesis 3:16**

Let's think about this picture for a moment:

A new life is formed. A baby is a new creation, abiding in the mother as he or she grows and develops. At first, the child looks nothing like their parents, but rather a nondescript blob. Then days and weeks pass by and this new life is transformed into the image of the parents. The baby does not have to strive to transform or survive; it must simply rest in the mother as she provides the nourishment and resources that it needs in order to grow. The child is perfectly content to abide in the mother's womb and receive all that it needs.

That is a picture of a new believer begotten of God. That believer is a child of God, a new creation. He or she is to abide in Christ as they grow and develop. At first, the new believer looks nothing like Christ; but as time goes by, we are transformed into the likeness of

God's Son. The believer does not have to work to transform or to survive; we must rest in Christ as He provides the nourishment and resources we need to grow in Him. We are to be perfectly content as we abide in Christ and receive all that we need for life and godliness.

Looking back to the beginning, when Adam and Eve sinned, God painted a new picture in childbirth. They were originally designed to abide in God and receive all that they needed for life and godliness, but when sin entered the world, they were expelled from the garden. They were disconnected from God as a child is forced to leave its mother and become disconnected from its life source in the womb. From that moment of birth, the child's flesh begins the dying process.

When a child is pushed from the womb, who is in more pain, the child or the mother? When Adam and Eve—created to abide in God—were expelled from the very presence of God, He placed upon the woman a curse that would picture what had just happened to them. Adam and Eve had at one time been content to abide in God, being nourished by Him. But now they must go. *It pained God far more to cut man off from His presence than it could ever hurt man.* As a newborn is severed from its mother, man had been severed from the presence of God.

Every time a doctor cuts a newborn's umbilical cord, he is literally picturing what happened to all of mankind. Woman's pain is multiplied, but it will never compare to what God went through in cutting off His beloved creation after they sinned.

A DISCONNECTED WORLD

Fast-forward to today. Mankind has been hungry since the days of Adam, trying to fill the voids in life. Sin is the result of man's attempt to satisfy and fill those various hungers/voids. Do you realize that Satan never misses an opportunity to take advantage of the hunger in our life?

Sometimes people say: "I am not that spiritual." This is a vague statement. Every person has a spirit, making every person a spiritual being. Scripture never uses the term *unspiritual.* An individual's spirit dies when separated from God, but that dead spirit is *quickened* (made alive) once in Christ. You are not spiritual or unspiritual, you are either spiritually alive (quickened) or spiritually dead in your sins. Decisions are spiritual either way. Therefore, your decisions contribute to your spiritual contentment or to your spiritual hunger.

It is interesting to note that Satan has never created anything, but he will provide substitutes to fill a void in our life, just as he did with Adam. Adam chose the forbidden fruit to satisfy his hunger and fill the void. It was not just a choice to satisfy his stomach, it was a spiritual choice and it led to disaster.

We all experience voids in our life at times. We can choose to fill the voids with the things of God and be truly satisfied, or we can fill them with the things that Satan has to offer.

Satan loves voids. After all, Jesus said that Satan came to steal, kill, and destroy. He never misses the opportunity to offer us something to fill the void. He wants to deceive us by manipulating our perception and make us believe that nothing is actually something. Satan loves emptiness!

DELIVER US FROM EMPTINESS

God despises emptiness! Jesus did not like empty nets, empty water pots, empty baskets, empty bellies, or empty hearts. In fact, Christ even taught that a man who is swept clean but left *empty* is vulnerable to demon possession. Everywhere he went, Jesus destroyed emptiness. He filled nets with fish, baskets with bread, and hearts with truth and hope. Christ did not even leave the grave empty; he wrapped and neatly folded his burial clothes up and left them inside the tomb.

Why does God hate emptiness so much? God hates emptiness because *emptiness is evil*; emptiness is a synonym for evil.

EMPTINESS IS EVIL?

How do we explain or comprehend the concept of evil? Many believers have no idea what evil really is or where it came from. God gives us the origin of evil. Surprise...He *actually* takes credit for it, but does so by explaining what evil actually *is.*

> I form the light, and create darkness:
> I make peace, and create evil:
> I the LORD do all these things.
> **Isaiah 45:7**

God gives us a direct parallel to help us understand evil. To understand evil, consider darkness. God created light, and when light was created, the potential for darkness existed immediately. The removal of light causes darkness.

Darkness, then, is not a something; it is the ***absence*** of a something.

The word ***darkness*** is simply a term used to describe the absence of light. We can study light, but not darkness. In fact, we can use Newton's prism to break white light into many colors and study the various wavelengths of each color. You cannot measure darkness. A simple ray of light can illuminate a world of darkness. How can you know the darkness of a certain space? You measure the amount of light present.

Therefore, darkness is a term used by man to describe what happens when there is no light present. Likewise, God's presence brings with it peace and goodness. The absence of God's peace and goodness is what God calls evil.

Evil is the scriptural word that describes the *emptiness* that exists in the *absence* of God's peaceful presence. Evil has no existence of its own. It is really the lack of God's closeness and peace.

For example, what happens when you remove a bucket of dirt from the ground? We call the absence of missing dirt, a hole in the ground. The hole cannot be separated from the ground where it exists. You cannot pick the hole up and put it in your pocket. The hole in the ground is real, but it only exists in the ground. Emptiness can only exist when something has been removed.

Everything that God creates is good, but in His absence is evil. Evil is the opposite of good and the absence of peace. *Evil is a painful nothingness.* The absence of truth is evil. The absence of hope is evil. **Evil is the void of God's presence.**

The Hollywood movie *Star Wars* tries to portray evil as a force, but in reality, the opposite is true.

Wickedness is a force because it is a something.

Sin is a force because it is a something.

Iniquity is a force because it is a something.

But not evil—evil is not a force; it is the absence of a something.

Evil is a void, an emptiness that will kill you. Like a fish out of water, mankind goes mad, gasping for something and receiving nothing. Why are so many people suffering? It's not a *something* that's wrong—it's an *emptiness* that's wrong. Again, **voids are EVIL**.

Evil is spiritual darkness.
Evil is spiritual hunger.
Evil is spiritual vanity.
Evil is spiritual voids.
Evil is spiritual hate.
Evil is spiritual fear.
Evil is spiritual laziness.
Evil is spiritual thirst.
Evil is spiritual deafness.
Evil is spiritual emptiness.
Evil is spiritual lust.
Evil is spiritual covetousness.
Evil is spiritual blindness.
Evil is spiritual death.

These things are the domain of the devil. Satan does not rule over *a something*, he rules over voids. **Voids** are his domain.

The Word of God says in Ephesians that he is the *ruler of the darkness*. Realize that the darkness is the absence of light. He is the prince of the power *of the air*. What do you have with a box full of air? You have a box full of nothingness. Satan has no legal right to anything; he rules the void.

DELIVERANCE FROM EVIL

The man who stumbles in darkness is much different from the man who runs away from the light. The stumbling of a man born blind is not a sin. Why, because God allowed his blindness. Stumbling is a natural result of one who walks without sight and assistance. This is why it is important to understand that no child is born *with* sin.

BEWARE OF HUNGER

Sin is the transgression of the law (1 John 3:4). Sin is knowing to do good, but choosing not to do it (James 4:17). Which law has the newborn transgressed? If there is no transgression, then it is not sin. An infant is born innocent of any transgression; however, born into a disconnected, darkened world—a world cut off from the source of Life. In the absence of God's light, darkness abounds. Those without Christ are blinded by this darkness. All of mankind needs the Light.

Do we truly believe that the lost are spiritually blind? God's Word says they are blind, but do we treat them as blind people? How did Jesus treat the blind? A man who is blinded by the darkness needs the light. A blind man needs compassion and help. How did Jesus treat the spiritually blind? Jesus had compassion. He delivered them from their blindness. Do we have His compassion? Do we show them how to be delivered from their blindness?

When Jesus taught His disciples to pray, one of the petitions He instructed them to make was to ask God to deliver them from evil.

> And lead us not into temptation, but **deliver us from evil**: For thine is the kingdom, and the power, and the glory, for ever. Amen.
> **Matthew 6:13**

He did not tell us to seek deliverance from sin, iniquity, or transgression because evil is the void in which all of those "somethings" reside. Seeking deliverance from evil will destroy the void in which sin resides.

Destroying the hole will get rid of the trash that has filled the hole. Too often, many believers become obsessed with attacking the trash and ignoring the void. Sin and iniquity are undoubtedly trash, but if we only remove the trash and leave the void, Satan will try again to fill the void with trash. There will always be room for trash and the war against trash will never end. Acknowledge the trash, but do not become a professional trash-attacker. Destroy the void by filling it with the things of God and there will be no place for trash.

The goodness of God cannot be questioned. He has given us so much to enjoy, yet man still succumbs to voids.

In my counseling, I have discovered that most people become addicted to a particular sin because they are attempting to fill some kind of void. I love introducing people to this truth. God not only cleanses them from all of their trash, He also delivers them from every spiritual void.

CHAPTER 3

TO DO OR NOT TO DO
(THAT IS THE COMMANDMENT)

FEEDING THE HUNGRY SOUL

TO DO OR NOT TO DO

Adam and Eve were made in the image of God. This does not mean that their height, hair color, or skin tone reflected that of God's. They were created as *triune* beings. God made the angels who were self-aware and could exercise reason. They could choose to obey or disobey, but they were *not* triune. The angels were created as spiritual, one-dimensional creatures. God made the animals, too, who could exercise feelings and emotion, but they were unable to reason and make moral choices. They were two-dimensional creatures.

God said to Himself, of Himself: *"Let **us** make man in **our** image, after **our** likeness..."* (Genesis 1:26)

The Hebrew word for God in Genesis chapter one is Elohim, which means Triunity. Mankind was unique—created with body, soul, and spirit. This triunity of man is the perfect reflection of God's triunity—The Father, Son, and Holy Spirit. In reality, man does not have a soul—man *is* a soul—man's soul has a spirit and body.

God created the soul and covered the soul with humus, which is dirt. This is how we derive the term *human*. However, this soul covered in dirt was not yet alive. Then God breathed His Spirit into the soul and flesh body of man, which is the light of our conscience. That breath—God's breath—made the soul alive.

> So God created man in His own image, in the image of God created He him; male and female created He them.
> **Genesis 1:27**

Creation was God expanding his Kingdom. Earth was like a new colony, where mankind, both male and female would rule and care for creation together. In the new colonized Earth, God walked with mankind. Adam and Eve did not use an altar. They did not need a temple or a priest. They enjoyed a personal, one-on-one relationship with The Almighty.

They ruled under the care of their Creator.

> And God said, Let us make man in our image, after our likeness; and let **THEM** have dominion…
> **Genesis 1:26a**

God established Earth and gave mankind authority over it. By the way, notice God said **"them."** Both male and female were given dominion. The word *kingdom* is actually a compound word derived from two words: king and dominion. Adam and Eve were dignitaries. They were royalty. *Mankind was truly created for the kingdom life.* We foolishly exchanged our scepter for sin. One day Christ will reestablish His physical kingdom on Earth and the redeemed will rule with Him once again. This is why He is called the *"King of **kings**."* Mankind was given the authority to take care of creation and each other.

POWER VERSUS AUTHORITY

Man still longs for control. We think and say things like, "I am going to live *my* life *my* way." The problem with that thought process is that we lack power. We always have lacked power. This is so important to understand. Even from the beginning, mankind has always been powerless. God bequeathed to us the *authority* to rule, but He alone holds the *power*. *Authority without power is like a well without water.* All of man's authority came from God.

Have you ever wondered why God did not intervene when Lucifer was tempting man? Why didn't God slap the fruit out of Adam's hand? After all, as a parent, I would slap the fork out of my child's hand if she were heading toward the power outlet. So why didn't God stop Adam from eating the fruit?

TO DO OR NOT TO DO

God exercises His power on Earth through the authority of man. The reason God would not intervene is simple; God will not violate His Word. For God to impose His power on Earth *without* the conduit of man's authority would be contrary to what *He established* in creation, and therefore an illegal action.

This is why God always exercises His interventional power on Earth through the conduit of human authority. For example, Moses had the authority to cross over the Red Sea on dry ground, but only God had the power to part the sea. This is also what makes the incarnation of Christ so amazingly wonderful! The Son of God wrapped himself in the flesh of man and was born into humanity—Emmanuel—God in man. *Jesus was the first man ever to have both authority and power.*

If you've ever wondered why we also must pray, now you know. We pray, exercising our authority; God answers, exercising His power. **Prayer is the authority of man tapping into the power of God.** Jesus said, *"Whatsoever ye bind on earth, shall be bound in Heaven: and whatsoever ye shall loose on earth shall be loosed in Heaven"* (Matthew 18:18). Authority was given to man, but we are powerless without God.

Along with man's authority, God gave some commands. His commands are His expectations. They are not passive—they demand active obedience.

God placed man in a special garden within Eden and gave him a two-fold command. First, He commanded him to avoid hunger. "And The Lord God *commanded* the man, saying, of every tree of the garden thou mayest *freely* eat". Notice the word *freely*, which means to indulge.

God commanded Adam to eat *all* he could eat. That's a pretty cool command, don't you think? It was also a super important command.

Think about it, if Adam had followed this positive command, he might never have fallen. He could have told Eve, "I am sorry honey, but I am stuffed." He could have *avoided* the temptation instead of trying to resist it, if he tried to *resist* at all.

If Adam had followed God's positive (*to do*) command to indulge on the permitted fruit, then it would have been easy to follow God's negative (*not to do*) command to abstain from the forbidden fruit. It is really simple logic.

I want to introduce you to a pattern within God's Word that is essential in avoiding spiritual hunger and eliminating voids.

Notice the sequence of God's commands. God's "thou shalt" commandments are of a higher priority than His "thou shalt not" commandments. Read that last sentence again.

In fact, *obeying* His "Do" commands, eradicates the *need* for His "Do Not" commands.

Consider the Ten Commandments:

*Thou shalt have **no** other gods before me.*
***Thou shalt not** make unto thee any graven image.*
***Thou shalt not** take the name of the Lord thy God in vain.*
***Thou shalt not** kill.*
***Thou shalt not** commit adultery.*
***Thou shalt not** steal.*
***Thou shalt not** bear false witness.*
***Thou shalt not** covet.*

There are many "thou shalt not" commands in the law, yet Christ said there are two "thou shalt" commands on which **all** of the law hangs:

TO DO OR NOT TO DO

> **Thou shalt** love the Lord thy God with all thy heart,
> and with all thy soul, and with all thy mind.
> This is the first and great commandment.
>
> And the second is like unto it.
> **Thou shalt** love thy neighbor as thyself.
> On these two commandments
> hang ALL the law and the prophets.
> **Matthew 22:37-40**

Someone who is in love with God—completely satisfied in Him—will have no fear of committing idolatry or adultery. There will be no void in which that trash can dwell.

Adam was first commanded to indulge—to eat freely of *all* he could eat. Then God said, *"But of the tree of the knowledge of good and evil, **thou shalt not** eat of it."* This is the first "Do Not" command in Scripture.

FOR EXAMPLE

The first general order for every American Soldier says: "I will guard everything within the limits of my post and quit my post only when properly relieved." That is the Soldier's law. If a Soldier is commanded to stand guard all night and he abandons his post, does it matter how far away he goes? No, AWOL (Absence Without Official Leave) is still AWOL based on the fact that he abandoned his post. The Soldier who leaves his post and drives out of state is no worse than the one who leaves post to run to the convenience store; both of them abandoned their post. The consequences may be different as determined by the circumstances. Nevertheless, what makes him an unfit Soldier is not what he did after going AWOL, but the fact that he abandoned his post. The Army does not have the burden of commanding a Soldier on duty of every place he is not to go. The command to guard his post is sufficient. Likewise, obeying

God's "thou shalt" commandments would be sufficient, if we only obeyed them.

ABIDE IN CHRIST

Adam did not realize it at the time, but God's restriction on eating from the Tree of Knowledge was only temporary. We know this restriction was not permanent for a few reasons. First of all, God said in Hosea 4:6, *"My people are destroyed for **lack** of knowledge."* God desires for man to **gain** knowledge.

Secondly, the Tree of Knowledge was created by God and He said everything He created was "good." Psalm 84:11 states, *"The LORD will give grace and glory; **no good thing** will He withhold from them that walk uprightly."* Therefore, it is logical to conclude that God would have eventually *rewarded* Adam with fruit from this Tree of Knowledge if he walked in obedience.

Most importantly though, we know it was a temporary restriction because God said it was created for man to eat. Genesis 1:29 states: *"And God said, Behold, I have given you every herb bearing seed which is upon the face of all the earth, and **every tree**, in the which is the fruit of a tree yielding seed; to you it shall be for meat."* Had Adam simply been filled and willing to trust God's word, he would have surely enjoyed the fruit of the Tree of Knowledge eventually.

Adam was first commanded to indulge and avoid hunger. Only then was Adam commanded not to eat the fruit from the Tree of Knowledge. He was warned that if he disobeyed, he would die—yet Adam sinned.

Does this mean that a negative command beginning with "Thou shalt not" is wrong or unnecessary? No. We find present in nature a divine balance. Biology consists of the male and the female. Electricity functions and performs its work by use of both the

TO DO OR NOT TO DO

positive and the negative. Elements are either alkaline or acid. No law could be a perfect law unless it contains, in perfect balance, both positive and negative attributes.

However, trying to live life obeying *only* the commandments that begin with "Thou Shalt Not" would be a miserable existence. Nevertheless, it seems like some believers base their whole existence on what they "do not do." You are not a spiritual believer because you "do not drink" or "do not do drugs," or "do not fornicate." Even *unbelievers* abstain from certain sins. You are a spiritual believer when you *abide in Christ*—it is about obeying His positive command "*Abide.*" When we obey the positive command, the negative commands are automatically fulfilled in perfect balance.

The words *thou shall not* invokes obedience through fear while the words *thou shalt* invites obedience through love. *Both of the Thou Shalt commandments require love.* The *do not* commands of God require a man to conform through obligation, but the *do* commands of God transform a man through thanksgiving.

The voids that are created by *omission* in our lives influence the sins of *commission*. Adam did not know fear until he sinned. God's character demands obedience. Outside of His presence, there are literally hundreds of *do not* rules that always have a consequence. These rules inspire obedience through fear; however, as believers we are reconciled in Christ. The fear of the Lord may be the beginning of wisdom, but the end is love. Love is our hope, our goal, our sure destiny as believers.

> A **new** commandment I give unto you, That ye love one another; as I have loved you, that ye also love one another.
> John 13:34

FEEDING THE HUNGRY SOUL

CHAPTER 4

ABSENCE DEMANDS ATTENTION
(DESTROY THE VOID)

ABSENCE DEMANDS ATTENTION

God desires to destroy every void, but Satan offers his substitutes to fill the void. This is what David alluded to in Psalm 23 when he said: *"The LORD is my Shepherd, I shall **not** want."* In other words, if the LORD is your Shepherd, you will not have a hunger. Following Him, you will be delivered from evil and you will be filled.

When a void exists, it creates desires. *It becomes a vacuum, demanding to be filled.* Once we try to fill a void with the trash of this world, we are trapped in an endless cycle. We cannot get enough alcohol. We cannot get enough narcotics. We cannot get enough sex. We cannot get enough pleasure. The sinful pleasures of this world cannot destroy spiritual voids.

The problem is not simply what we do not have; the problem is in not realizing how much we *can* have. Adam's fulfillment was not in all that was given to him *by* God, but in all that he had in his relationship *with* God. The fullness Adam enjoyed in the Garden of Eden was not because of all that God had given to him. It was because of all that God was to him. The pleasures of the Garden of Eden were extensions of his relationship with God. It was the relationship that brought about the goodness.

So how was Satan able to convince Adam and Eve to disobey God and forfeit the goodness? He took advantage of their natural hunger, both physically and mentally.

Adam was given a smorgasbord of plenty and commanded to eat all he could eat. Satan strategically planned his attack when he knew they would be most vulnerable. Temptation is rife with vulnerability.

He also convinced them that God was withholding something from them. Satan even made a promise to them. He said: "If you eat this fruit, you will understand things that you have never understood before." The temptation was not only the fruit, but their *desire* for something that they were told was missing.

Was anything missing? Absolutely not!

Satan convinced them otherwise. What did he *want* them to believe was missing? He wanted them to believe that God was not allowing them to enjoy something. Make no mistake—they knew what was *right and wrong*. They had never *experienced* what was *good and evil*. Up to this point, all they knew was that which was good. All the creations of God were good. Satan was essentially saying that God doesn't want you to try the other side. It's like someone who tries to tempt you by saying, "you don't know what you are missing."

The very idea that you are missing something creates a ***void***.

When a void exists, we have a natural desire to fill it. We were not designed for emptiness. Trying to fill a void on our own is like trying to nail jelly to a tree; it is always an exercise in futility.

All sin begins when something is missing. Even believers face temptation when they are missing something. This always leads them to seek after something to fill the void. When in truth, any attempt you make to control your behavior is actually you being controlled *by* your behavior. **Uselessly trying to fill the voids in life is Satan's master deception**.

THE MASTER DECEIVER

Most believers are aware that Satan is a fallen cherub, but they are uncertain of the details behind his fall.

Satan was created as a cherub named Lucifer. The name Lucifer means "light-bearer" or "shining one." The words that God used to describe Lucifer when he was created are really amazing. God's Word tells us that Lucifer was the apex of perfection—he sealed up the sum—full of wisdom and perfect in beauty.

God had given Lucifer a specific role and position in heaven, but he became prideful as a result of the gifts that God had given him. Speaking to Lucifer in Ezekiel 28:5, God says: *"Thou **increased** thy riches, and thine heart is lifted up because of **thy** riches."* Lucifer became prideful and rebelled against God. As a result, God removed him from the unique position that had been given him.

It appears that Lucifer was the *first* to eat the forbidden fruit. Genesis 3:6 *"And when the woman **saw** the tree was good for food..."* How did Eve *see* that it was *good for food unless* Lucifer was eating it?

Lucifer desired knowledge. He lied to Eve with confidence, casting doubt on God's Word. You can imagine how easily he sowed this doubt—he is eating the fruit, and he is *not* dying. Then Lucifer told Eve that she and Adam would be like gods.

Notice carefully the words in Genesis 3:1-6. Lucifer asked Eve if God had specifically commanded *her* not to eat from the Tree of Knowledge, knowing full well that God had given the command to Adam *before* Eve was formed. Eve could *see* the fruit was good for food, and she *saw* that it was pleasant to her eyes, and she *saw* that it was desired to make one wise. Lucifer made a great spectacle of himself for Eve. Eve saw his desire for the fruit and she liked what she saw.

She took a bite—and didn't die...

Adam was there *with* Eve. God had previously told him that Eve was his wife and they were one flesh. He observed her conversation with Lucifer. He watched as she placed the forbidden fruit to her lips. He closely watched Eve take her first bite. Then nothing happened. Eve was still breathing. Eve was still standing. Eve was not dead. She handed the fruit to Adam and he took a bite. Instantly upon *Adam's disobedience*, both of their eyes were opened and they were sick with shame.

For the first time ever, man experienced fear, humiliation, and guilt. Then they vainly tried to hide from God. On that day, mankind was removed from Eden. Their walk with God in the cool of the day was over. Their peace, comfort, and spiritual connection with God were all destroyed.

Adam and Eve died that day—*spiritually*.

Man, for the first time, was disconnected from his life source—God.

Sure the *symptoms* of life remained, but if you uproot a plant from the soil, it is essentially dead. Even though it may bear the symptoms of life for a time, any living thing that is ripped from its life source will surely die.

GIVING SATAN A PLACE

Referring to Satan, Jesus said, *"When he speaketh a lie, he speaketh of his own: for he is a liar, and the father of it"* (John 8:44).

A void is not simply emptiness; it is an absence that demands attention. If you remove truth, *confusion* and *chaos* will ensue. Remove hope and the heart will be sickened. **One of the symptoms of having a spiritual void is the overwhelming need to fill it.** Satan knows this all too well and he is ready to assist. The flesh will always want more than it can have. So the shallow satisfaction of *having* is continuously replaced with more *wanting*.

ABSENCE DEMANDS ATTENTION

Friends, we often open the door for the devil ignorantly. Ephesians 4:27 says: *"Neither give **place** to the devil."* When Satan is given an opportunity to fill a void, he will cause total devastation. In John 10:10 we read that Satan comes to steal, kill, and destroy. We must be vigilant that we do not allow voids in our life for him to fill. When we have a void, we *give place* to the devil; he now has a place to do his work and to leave his trash. Watching and praying requires effort, but it is critical for our protection against the enemy. Saints, watching and praying is an antidote for ignorance. Remember, ignorance is no excuse.

There is never an excuse.

> Hope deferred maketh the heart sick:
> but when the desire cometh,
> it is a tree of life.
> **Proverbs 13:12**

FEEDING THE HUNGRY SOUL

CHAPTER 5

THE "MORAL" MAJORITY

FEEDING THE HUNGRY SOUL

THE "MORAL" MAJORITY

One of Satan's great deceptions is his ability to fill voids with *morality instead of spirituality.* If he cannot fill your void with *bad* things, he will gladly fill it with *good* things. The problem is that morality will damn a person faster than anything else. It is just a flavor of poison. A ship full of solid gold would certainly sink faster than a ship carrying dung. Similarly, a person's apparent morality does not indicate the reality of the heart. Morality is a standard of what a person does *not do*, unlike spirituality which is based on spiritual fullness in Christ.

This is why Satan's greatest tool against the gospel is religion. Religion makes great use of morality. Religion's focus is on what I do or don't do. The gospel's focus is on what Christ did. Religion produces pride and despair. The gospel produces humility and confidence. Religion is motivated by fear. The gospel is motivated by love. Being *moral* is not the same as being *spiritual*. Morality is a standard for good works. Spirituality is living and resting in the finished work of Christ.

I propose that the 1950's television show "Leave It To Beaver" could, in this sense, be a more dangerous show than the vulgarity we have today. It was the first show that presented a moral lesson in every episode, yet it is fully devoid of Christ. Being morally good without Christ is just as bankrupt as the filthy wickedness today, yet its moral beauty makes it more acceptable and alluring.

For certain, we should do good, obey and be examples of right living. But **Christ should always be our assurance instead of our insurance.** Our boast is in Christ ALONE and Him crucified.

What did Jesus call the religious, moral standard-bearers of His day? Well quite frankly, the Lord called them children of the devil. *"Ye are of your father the devil, and the lusts of your father ye will do. He was a murderer from the beginning, and abode not in the truth, because there is no truth in him. When he speaketh a lie, he speaketh of his own: for he is a liar, and the father of it."* John 8:44

Jesus did not mince words mind you, but **He never criticized anyone for whom He was not willing to die.**

BE YE SEPARATE—FROM WHAT?

Rather than watering down the straight forward language that our Lord used, I think it is best to actually understand what he is saying. Jesus was addressing the Pharisaical Jews.

The term Pharisee means "separatist." They took pride in separating from those whom they deemed less righteous, such as publicans. Are there any believers today separating themselves from those whom they deem unworthy? God's Word does admonish a form of separation. In 2 Corinthians 6:14-17 we read:

> [14] Be ye not unequally yoked together with unbelievers:
> for what fellowship hath righteousness with unrighteousness?
> and what communion hath light with darkness?
>
> [15] And what concord hath Christ with Belial?
> or what part hath he that believeth with an infidel?
>
> [16] And what agreement hath the temple of God with idols?
> for ye are the temple of the living God;
> as God hath said, I will dwell in them, and walk in them;
> and I will be their God, and they shall be my people.
>
> [17] Wherefore come out from among them,
> and be ye **SEPARATE**, saith the Lord,
> and touch not the unclean thing;
> and I will receive you.
> **2 Corinthians 6:14-17**

Who are the *unbelievers* that this passage references? In the context of chapters 5 and 6, the *unbelievers* are those who

THE "MORAL" MAJORITY

aggressively *refuse* the finished work of Christ. In other words, we are to separate ourselves from those people who reject Christ by continuing to rely and trust in their *own* self-righteousness and moral standards. Your flesh will never win points with God (read 2 Corinthians 5:11-21 below).

Our reconciliation to God is not accomplished by the works of the flesh. We cannot strive toward perfection. That's impossible. But once we have surrendered our works for his gift, we become Christ's ambassadors *IN* this world, but never *OF* this world. That is true separation. God does not command us to separate from blind men who need the Light, but to separate from the separatists who make morality their righteousness apart from Christ.

> [11] Knowing therefore the terror of the Lord, we persuade men;
> but we are made manifest unto God;
> and I trust also are made manifest in your consciences.
>
> [12] For we commend not ourselves again unto you,
> but give you occasion to glory on our behalf,
> that ye may have somewhat to answer them
> which glory in appearance, and not in heart.
>
> [13] For whether we be beside ourselves, it is to God:
> or whether we be sober, it is for your cause.
>
> [14] For the love of Christ constraineth us;
> because we thus judge,
> that if one died for all,
> then were all dead:
>
> [15] And that he died for all,
> that they which live should not henceforth live unto themselves,
> but unto him which died for them, and rose again.
>
> [16] Wherefore henceforth know we no man after the flesh:
> yea, though we have known Christ after the flesh,
> yet now henceforth know we him no more.

> [17] Therefore if any man be in Christ, he is a new creature:
> old things are passed away;
> behold, all things are become new.
>
> [18] And all things are of God,
> who hath reconciled us to himself by Jesus Christ,
> and hath given to us the ministry of reconciliation;
>
> [19] To wit, that God was in Christ,
> reconciling the world unto himself,
> not imputing their trespasses unto them;
> and hath committed unto us the word of reconciliation.
>
> [20] Now then we are ambassadors for Christ,
> as though God did beseech you by us:
> we pray you in Christ's stead,
> be ye reconciled to God.
>
> [21] For he hath made him to be sin for us, who knew no sin;
> that we might be made the righteousness of God in him.
> **2 Corinthians 5:11-21**

THE MODERN PHARISEE

Satan's masterpiece isn't the prostitute; it's the Pharisee. Jesus called them white-washed tombs. Jesus was calling them out for their emptiness.

> Woe unto you, scribes and Pharisees, hypocrites!
> for ye are like unto whited sepulchres,
> which indeed appear beautiful outward,
> but are within full of dead men's bones,
> and of all uncleanness.
> **Matthew 23:27**

Man does not ascend from the muck of wickedness and ignorance toward morality. He descends from the truth of God to the muck of morality, which is self-righteousness. The religion of good works is

THE "MORAL" MAJORITY

man wallowing in the pit. That is man's lowest state. He falls from the truth of God to the slime of religion. Religion is not man at his highest; it is man at his lowest. Religion is the filthiest trash Satan ever throws in a void. The gospel destroys the emptiness of religion.

Sadly, we are dealing with the exact same separatist attitude in our churches today that Christ experienced with the Pharisees. Modern *Christians* are quick to plaster a fish on their car, snap a WWJD bracelet on their wrist, and ignore the rest of the world.

Just because someone calls themselves a *professing Christian* does not mean they are truly trusting in the finished work of Christ.

It's sad, but true, many have enlisted in some morality program where they must abstain from *this* and do *that* to please God. Essentially, they are trying to save themselves. Jesus did not come to educate men and women on the values of avoiding bad behavior and strategies for better scholarship. Jesus came to resurrect dead men. Salvation isn't about bad people behaving better; it's about dead people being made alive.

This world is full of moral taskmasters who are ready to pounce on anyone who fails to worship their idol of high morality. Understand, the Pharisees were worshipping a god of their own making—a god of fear, legalism, and judgment—a false image of God. Their false image didn't give two cents about the lost and dying world around them. Their false image couldn't care less about the widows and orphans.

The false god of Phariseeism is distant and unconcerned. Their *god* is ready to crush anyone at a moment's notice for the smallest infraction of their own traditions and manmade laws.

The Pharisees were appalled at the notion of a God who genuinely cared about sinners. They *refused* to even acknowledge the God who showed mercy to *hookers*! The Pharisees were not worshipping *our Father who art in heaven.*

No doubt, the Pharisees had great morals. They had beautiful traditions. They had fantastic reputations, but they outright rejected Jesus. The Pharisees prided themselves on their good deeds and scripture memorizations, but none of that is experiential evidence of knowing the truth. A man can memorize all the ingredients required for making buttered biscuits, but until he takes a bite into one, he'll remain clueless about their flavor and goodness. Those religious moralists refused Christ, and were unknowingly worshiping *Diabolos*—the devil himself—and Jesus called them children of the devil. (John 8:44)

So, why does Jesus refer to Satan as the Pharisees' big daddy? Satan was the first murderer of grace and the founder of every lie. In the same way that the founders of nations are called founding *fathers*, the Devil is the *father* of all deception that we call self-righteousness. Satan is the father behind the works of the flesh. Satan is the prince of darkness, and his religion is blind *moral* leaders leading the blind.

Jesus came unto his own and his own received Him not. He was the LIGHT, but the religious moral separatists couldn't see the light. They preferred the *artificial* light of self-righteousness. It is usually easy to spot these religious taskmasters. They all share the common fruit of self-righteousness: burnout, depression, no sense of humor, no creativity, legalism, insecurity, fear, criticism, paranoia, pride, arrogance, false humility, separatism, etc.

The fears and insecurities behind every false image of God are satanic. Even if they call the false image *Jesus*, if our morality is the standard in place of Christ's righteousness, then grace is reduced to nothing less than an airbrushed image of Satan himself.

THE "MORAL" MAJORITY

ALL HAVE SINNED

Another one of Satan's crafty deceptions is his ability to draw our attention to a particular sin and away from the void that harbors it. The man who forsakes church to play golf is no different than the man who forsakes church to fornicate. The void is not in where he *is*, but where he is ***not***. We are commanded not to forsake the assembling of ourselves together.

Remember the illustration of a soldier abandoning his post? If he abandoned his post to help old people in a nursing home instead of going to a bar to get drunk, does it matter? Of course not. He abandoned his post. There may be additional consequences if he also got drunk and brawled, but that sin would only have occurred because he failed to obey the command he was given.

The Pharisee does not grasp this principle because we ***all*** have abandoned our post, falling short of the Glory of God. We ***all***, like sheep, have gone astray.

Notice that even the city of Sodom was not destroyed because of the *presence* of sexual perversion, but because of her *lack* of righteousness. Sexual perversion would not have been rampant if righteousness had been present. Abandoning righteousness was her void, and sexual perversion is what filled that void. God did not promise to spare the city if they had ten fewer perverts, but rather if He found ten righteous to be present.

THE GOAL

> And he said to them all,
> If any man will come after me,
> let him deny himself,
> and take up his cross daily,
> and follow me.
> **Luke 9:23**

Please note: the goal isn't to take up the cross. The goal isn't to deny yourself. The goal is to follow Christ, wherever He goes.

So often we make the *giving up* of something, self-denial, or *cross bearing* the litmus of our faith. This is ludicrous and leads to Phariseeism. Men do not race for the sake of sweating; they race for the trophy. Likewise, to know Christ more, and the fellowship of His suffering, **is** our trophy.

CHAPTER 6

THE PURSUIT *of* HAPPINESS

THE PURSUIT OF HAPPINESS

Everyone wants to find happiness, and certainly, God has the answer to that pursuit. That being said, there are times when mourning is necessary and sadness is most appropriate. We often try to escape sadness when it may be necessary for God to work in that moment.

Ecclesiastes 3:4 expresses a season for every emotion, *"A time to weep, and a time to laugh; a time to mourn, and a time to dance."*

The book of Ecclesiastes was penned by King Solomon, the third king of Israel. He was the son of King David and Bathsheba, ruling through the golden age of Israel. He was the wisest, richest, and most powerful man of his time. His wisdom was spoken of all over the earth. His wealth was far beyond imagination, and he had every worldly desire at his fingertips: wine, women, and wealth.

Solomon tells us how he set out to determine man's purpose in living:

> And I gave my heart to seek and search out
> by wisdom concerning **all** things that are done **under** heaven:
> this sore travail hath God given to the sons of man
> to be exercised therewith.
> **Ecclesiastes 1:13**

Solomon carefully describes the different ways in which he pursued happiness.

Solomon penned the books of Proverbs and Ecclesiastes. The book of Proverbs records his wisdom, and the book of Ecclesiastes graphically records his unhappy life. For the counselor who seeks to give scriptural counsel, I don't think there are two greater books in God's Word. Notice, the key word in Ecclesiastes is **vanity.** The entire book of Ecclesiastes shows us the *emptiness* found in one's pursuit of worldly happiness.

VEXATION OF SPIRIT

Solomon's words are so pertinent because multitudes go to their graves every day, having TRIED (rather unsuccessfully) to live a life of happiness.

After everything God gave Solomon, he was still hungry for something. Solomon tried to fill his void by worshipping Ashtoreth, the goddess of sex. Solomon neglected God and not only lost his kingdom, but failed in his search for happiness. Solomon died a dejected, sick, old man.

Why didn't his wisdom, wealth, and power make him happy?

What caused Solomon's downfall?

> For all that is in the world,
> the **lust** of the flesh,
> and the **lust** of the eyes,
> and the **pride** of life,
> is not of the Father, but is of the world.
> **1 John 2:16**

You will notice that Solomon's contempt wasn't because of a *something*, but rather the lack of *something*. He had a lust, a hunger to fill emptiness. Vanity is emptiness.

Another phrase Solomon uses throughout his writings is "vexation of spirit." The word vexation expresses his dissatisfaction with life and a longing for something real. When Solomon summed up his life, nothing he accomplished filled the longing void in his spirit.

Solomon explains:

THE PURSUIT OF HAPPINESS

> I have seen all the works that are done <u>under</u> the sun;
> and, behold, all is vanity and vexation of spirit.
> **Ecclesiastes 1:14**

Some of the richest men on earth are also some of the loneliest and unhappiest people. Many die with no family or friends by their side. Solomon concluded: "All of this is vanity and vexation of spirit."

Many men, like Solomon, strive within themselves their whole lives to feel something, although they are not sure what. It is not always the case, but some short men wish they were tall. Tall men wish they were not so tall. Fat men wish they were thin. Thin men wish they could put on weight. Bald men wish they had hair. Some men who have hair shave their heads. Women who are blond dye their hair dark. Brunette ladies want to be blond, and so on.

Men and women recklessly search for perfect happiness.

In his wisdom, Solomon knew all these strivings are normal in mankind. To desire something is normal, but to pursue that as your source of happiness is vanity. Even Solomon could not find the answer as to why these things vexed his spirit. Why couldn't he just find happiness?

> I said in mine heart,
> Go to now, I will prove thee with mirth,
> therefore enjoy pleasure:
> and, behold, this also is vanity.
> **Ecclesiastes 2:1**

Solomon tried *everything* to satisfy the longing in his heart. To feel happy in his life, he tried mirth. The word mirth means: joy, gladness, and pleasure. Many kings surrounded themselves with *jesters* who could make them laugh. They surrounded themselves at court with every pleasurable pastime. But alas, Solomon eventually discovered that constant laughter and pleasures never fulfilled the longing in his heart.

Today the world is full of comedians. Quite frankly, they are often some of the unhappiest, most unfulfilled people on earth. Many comics turn to sex, vulgarity and eventually to every perversion imaginable, where *anything goes* to get a laugh. But, all the laughs and applause in the world soon become hollow noise in the perverted ears of the audience. Most of these comedians discover, as did Solomon, that their life is "vanity and vexation of spirit," and they are found wanting. It is sad.

In Solomon's unquenchable thirst for happiness, he sent ships all over the world to search out magnificent treasures. No expense was too great and no distance was too far away to obtain anything that would bring delight to his heart and keep him entertained. All the women, entertainment, wealth, and luxury could not satisfy his spirit.

> [9] So I was great, and increased more
> than all that were before me in Jerusalem:
> also my wisdom remained with me.
>
> [10] And whatsoever mine eyes desired
> I kept not from them,
> I withheld not my heart from any joy;
> for my heart rejoiced in all my labour:
> and this was my portion of all my labour.
> **Ecclesiastes 2:9-10**

How did Solomon feel about all his great achievements? Sadly, even with all Solomon accomplished, in the end he declared they were all just vanity and vexation of spirit. In despair, Solomon cried out:

THE PURSUIT OF HAPPINESS

> "Therefore I **hated** life;
> because the work that is wrought under the sun
> is grievous unto me:
> for all is vanity and vexation of spirit.
> **Ecclesiastes 2:17**

Solomon hated his life. All his great accomplishments only left him lonely and unfulfilled. All his works seemed like nothing to him. He truly felt all things he did were vanity and vexed his spirit. Why did he feel this way?

> [18] Yea, I hated all my labour which I had taken under the sun: **because** I should leave it unto the man that shall be after me.
>
> [19] And who knoweth whether he shall be a wise man or a fool? Yet shall he have rule over all my labour wherein I have laboured,
> and wherein I have shewed myself wise under the sun.
> This is also vanity.
> **Ecclesiastes 2:18-19**

Solomon hated his life because he had lived it focused on the temporary. His life was spent chasing that which is *under the sun*. He chased happiness and found nothingness. Everything under the sun will perish.

Understanding Solomon's tormented soul helps us to better understand the tormented souls of people today.

GREATER THAN SOLOMON

Like Solomon, many people today seem unable to find contentment. Paul wrote to the young man Timothy:

> But godliness with contentment is great gain.
> **1 Timothy 6:6**

FEEDING THE HUNGRY SOUL

It has been approximately three thousand years since Solomon left the earth, yet mankind still has not learned the message he left for the world. Many homes in America have at least one copy of God's Word. Because of this, we have more wisdom at our fingertips than Solomon, yet many souls are just as tortured as Solomon's. We do not need to make the same mistakes, but many do—only to find out it's all vanity and vexation of spirit.

> The queen of the south shall rise up
> in the judgment with this generation,
> and shall condemn it:
> for she came from the uttermost parts of the earth
> to hear the wisdom of Solomon;
> and, behold a greater than Solomon is here.
> **Matthew 12:42**

What could the Queen of Sheba witness against this generation? What she saw in Solomon's house was the exact opposite of the life Jesus lived.

Jesus is greater than Solomon. Solomon had a great house. Jesus did not even own a house. Solomon had many servants. Jesus was a servant. Solomon had many riches. The only thing Jesus owned was the robe He wore. Solomon had a standing army and a navy with many ships. Jesus had twelve apostles and one of them was a traitor. Solomon had seven hundred wives and three hundred concubines. Jesus was a faithfully unmarried preacher, yet He was greater than Solomon.

So what could the Queen of Sheba witness against the wicked and adulterous generation of our day? She could condemn it because most of the world today desires to have what Solomon had *instead of* what Jesus had. Instead of serving, we want servants. Instead of prayer, we want protests and boycotts. Instead of seeking the eternal

THE PURSUIT OF HAPPINESS

Kingdom, we seek temporary happiness. Solomon's words should be read to every man who is trying to pursue happiness.

How should we pursue happiness? To answer this question, we have to look to the one who is greater than Solomon. When Jesus uses the word **blessed**; it often means **happy**. Jesus said: *"It is **more blessed** to give than to receive" (Acts 20:35).* For example, I love a good Snickers® bar. It makes me happy. If I pursue the candy bar and eat it, I may be happy temporarily. The next morning; however, I may get on the scale and conclude the Snickers® bar was nothing more than vanity and vexation of spirit.

If I pursue a Snickers® bar to give it away to someone else who loves them as I do, I will still wake up the next morning having given it away. Every day for the rest of my life, I can enjoy the happiness brought by giving it away and that enjoyment will continue.

The happiness brought by selfish consumption is temporary and vain, but the happiness brought by selflessly giving it away will last. It brings me more happiness to give than to receive. So my pursuit of happiness should not be in *my happiness*, but in the happiness of *others*. In this way, happiness is not temporary, but eternal. Truly, *"it is more blessed to give than to receive."*

ically ill and are unable to feed themselves.

CHAPTER 7

AVOIDING HUNGER

AVOIDING HUNGER

The Devil loves to fill voids. Even Jesus was no exception to Satan's *pattern* of temptation. In Matthew 4, we see that Satan came to our Lord in the wilderness after he had fasted for forty days and forty nights.

> [1] Then was Jesus led up of the Spirit
> into the wilderness to be tempted of the devil.
>
> [2] And when he had fasted forty days and forty nights,
> he was afterward an **hungred**.
> **Matthew 4:1-2**

Watch very carefully what Satan attempted to do to our Lord. First, Satan tried to fill a natural void in his *flesh* by appealing to his hunger.

> And when the tempter came to Him,
> he said, if thou be the Son of God,
> command that these stones be made bread.
> **Matthew 4:3**

Jesus was hungry, but He knew that all He had to do was call on His Father to be fed. Because He was living in the fullness of God, He was able to respond to Satan.

> But he answered and said,
> It is written, Man shall not live by bread alone,
> but by every word that proceedeth out of the mouth of God.
> **Matthew 4:4**

Next Satan tried to *create and fill* a void in His *faith* by testing whether God would protect Him from danger.

> [5] Then the devil taketh him up into the holy city,
> and setteth him on a pinnacle of the temple,

> [6] And saith unto him,
>   If thou be the Son of God, cast thyself down:
>   for it is written, He shall give his angels charge concerning thee:
>   and in their hands they shall bear thee up,
>   lest at any time thou dash thy foot against a stone.
>   **Matthew 4:5-6**

Sometimes, as we walk in the fullness of God's promises, we are tempted to fill a void of faith. We may attempt to *prove God* by our courage. We must always remember that the fullness of God will carry us through trials, but God does not have to prove His fullness.

> Jesus said unto him, It is written again,
> Thou shalt not tempt the Lord thy God.
> **Matthew 4:7**

Christ did not need to fill a void in His faith because there was no void. God has equipped every believer with the sustenance necessary for defeating Satan. Sometimes people worry about their propensity to doubt, but even the ability to doubt is a gift from God. Unfortunately, we use it in the wrong way. We should doubt the lies we hear and never the truth. Abiding in God's Word gives us the ability to know the difference.

Finally, Satan attempted to *create and fill* a void in his ***favor***.

> [8] Again, the devil taketh him up
> into an exceeding high mountain,
> and sheweth him all the kingdoms of the world,
> and the glory of them;
>
> [9] And saith unto him,
> All these things will I give thee,
> if thou wilt fall down and worship me.
> **Matthew 4:8-9**

AVOIDING HUNGER

Notice that Satan offered to give Jesus what He had already been promised. There was no void in His favor with God because He knew the promises of God. He knew *"The earth is the Lord's, and the fulness thereof; the world, and they that dwell therein"* (Psalm 24:1). Therefore, Jesus answered Satan with the following:

> Get thee hence, Satan: for it is written,
> Thou shalt worship the Lord thy God,
> and him only shalt thou serve.
> **Matthew 4:10**

Idolatry may occur as we seek to find favor that is missing in our lives. In an effort to feel better about ourselves, we worship things that cannot give us favor. Believers are not immune to this form of idolatry. We allow Satan to steal from us the promises of God, and a void is created. He then offers to us his version of what we have already been promised in Christ.

For example, Satan can offer religious busywork that causes us to miss our rest in Christ. We attempt to fill the void with religious activities such as teaching Sunday School or serving as a deacon. As a result, we could turn our spiritual gift into an idol.

> Then the devil leaveth him, and, behold,
> angels came and ministered unto him.
> **Matthew 11:11**

Afterward Jesus received the tender care of the angels. They did not come to fill a void for Christ, but demonstrated God's love to always take care of his own. Jesus won. Satan's temptations failed. We have the same Spirit of God within us.

Satan is still in the void-making and void-filling business. He will try to fill your void *with bad or with good, just so long as your void remains.* God is not interested in simply filling your void; God wants to destroy your void.

It is interesting to note that God was never responsible for bringing sin or iniquity upon a nation, but He did bring evil—a result of His **absence**, due to their rebellion.

Satan takes up residence where evil exists. Satan *fills the void* with wickedness, sins, perversions, and all manner of abominations.

God did not say: "Because of sin, my people perish." He said: "*My people are destroyed for their **lack** of knowledge*" (Hosea 4:6). God said it was the absence of something (knowledge) that caused His people to perish. The problem was and still is the void—the nothingness.

Similarly, Paul did not say: "In my flesh dwells perversions." He said: "*In my flesh dwelleth no good thing*" (Romans 7:18). Again we find an absence, nothingness, a a void where sin can reside. That is the problem.

When Abraham stood before the Lord on behalf of Sodom, it wasn't the presence of the sin of sodomy that brought forth judgment. It was the **absence** of righteousness.

God's truth and hope always produce peace, and the absence of that peace is evil.

Again, evil is a spiritual nothingness.

TRASH IN THE VOID

Jesus taught the disciples to pray," Deliver *us from evil.*" Why? The more you understand why, the more obvious it becomes; Satan loves to fill voids. We need to seek deliverance from every void in our life, wherein all manner of trash gets placed.

AVOIDING HUNGER

Every home makes trash, but not every home keeps it. When we hoard trash, our identity can be lost in the junk. Imagine digging a hole and filling it up with garbage. Would the hole still exist? Certainly, it would; only now, it would be filled with trash. That's what Satan does: he fills spiritual voids with trash.

The trash is the sin, transgressions, wicked labels, and iniquities that people exercise. Trash is something. Jesus knows that if we do not have the void, we will not collect the trash. Where the law said do not commit adultery, Jesus says do not lust. The lust *is* the hunger and emptiness. It is this void that Satan eventually fills with an adulterous relationship. If there is *no* lust, there is no place for adultery. If there is no void, there is no place for the trash.

Jacob, whose name means deceiver, stole Esau's birthright by taking advantage of Esau's hunger. Satan (our deceiver) is always ready to take advantage of our hunger.

Just like Adam, God creates each person spiritually whole, not incapable of sin but perfectly whole: body, soul, and spirit.

We are all born into a disconnected, empty world. Our present world is *separated* from God. At the point in time when we understand good and choose not to obey that which is good, we transgress the law of God.

> Therefore to him that **knoweth** to do good,
> and doeth it not, to him it is sin.
> **James 4:17**

Once we come to the knowledge of our responsibility to obey God and then we disobey knowing that we are transgressing His law, our spirit dies.

> ⁷ What shall we say then?
> Is the law sin? God forbid.
> Nay, I had not known sin, but by the law:
> for I had not known lust, except the law had said,
> Thou shalt not covet.
>
> ⁸ But sin, taking occasion by the commandment,
> wrought in me all manner of concupiscence.
> For without the law sin was dead.
>
> ⁹ For I was alive without the law once:
> but when the commandment came,
> sin revived, and I died."
> **Romans 7:7-9**

The spirit of man is the candle of the Lord (Proverbs 20:27). What is this candle? What is that light? We are told that Jesus is that light which lights every man who comes into the world (John 1:9). Every man who comes into the world has this light. But when we are confronted with the knowledge of our transgression, taught to us by the law, that candle goes dark.

> Because that, when they (mankind) knew God,
> they glorified him not as God, neither were thankful;
> but became vain in their imaginations,
> and their foolish heart was darkened.
> **Romans 1:27**

The heart of man was at one time lighted, but it then became darkened. The knowledge of sin, which comes by the law of God, slew the spirit of man. It put out the candle and darkened the heart. No longer whole, sin leaves us broken and no longer bearing the true image of a Holy God.

We are ***all*** born into a natural world filled with sin and ***separated*** from God; our only source of life. We allow Satan to multiply our voids creating a vacuum that alienates us from God. Attempting to fill the voids in our life, we are never satisfied. The search for pleasure to fill the voids is never-ending. The voids must be destroyed, and only God can destroy the void.

AVOIDING VERSUS RESISTING

On July 28, 1976, when most people were in their deepest slumber, an earthquake measuring 7.8 on the Richter Scale leveled the city of Tangshan. Hundreds of thousands were killed and many more injured. In only 14 seconds a reported 655,000 people perished in the area. How in the world did that many people lose their lives in only 14 seconds? Unbeknownst to the people of Tangshan, the ground beneath their feet had been shifting for decades. The tectonic plates were moving and the foundation had been eroding for nearly a century. Then one day, the earth shook.

God's Word tells us, *"If the foundations be destroyed, what can the righteous do?"* (Psalm 11:35). You see, their lack of knowledge concerning the imminent danger along that fault line cost hundreds of thousands of lives. How many lives could have been spared if only they had possessed that knowledge?

> Brethren, if a man be overtaken in a fault,
> ye which are spiritual,
> restore such an one in the spirit of meekness;
> considering thyself, lest thou also be tempted.
> **Galatians 6:1**

Look carefully at the passage of Galatians 6:1. It does not say, "If a man be overtaken **by** a fault." It says, *"If a man be overtaken **in** a fault."* A spiritual fault is not a euphemism such as a child blaming another sibling for something they did wrong. Rather, the scriptural understanding of a fault is the fault line beneath our feet.

Faults are not necessarily the sin that overtakes a person. Faults are weaknesses in our foundation. They are areas in one's life where he might lack the character he ought to have. A fault is what one falls *into* and becomes overtaken by sin.

When someone sins, it is the result of ignoring the fault line in their foundation. When we help each other with our faults, we help each other avoid sin.

For example, if a person is predisposed to being lazy, that is a fault. Laziness can cause someone to forsake the assembly of God's people. That is a sin. If a person is accountable for their faults, forsaking the assembly will not be a problem. Many sins are the result of faults not being confessed.

In our Lord's conversation with Peter, He told Peter that he would deny Him. Peter was overconfident—that was his fault line, not his sin. He later fell in that fault and was overtaken by the sin of denying the Lord. The Lord never berated Peter for having that fault line; rather, He warned Peter of the sin that would overtake him in that fault. We all have faults and as a result, we are vulnerable.

With that understanding, we are told to confess our *faults*, not our sins.

> Confess your faults one to another,
> and pray one for another,
> that ye may be healed.
> **James 5:16**

By sharing our faults, we seek strength and help in those weaknesses so that we do not stumble in that fault and become overtaken by a sin.

If we let those with whom we are intimately involved know our faults, then we can help each other. ***It is easier to avoid temptation***

than it is to resist temptation. I can avoid the fall if I can avoid the fault line.

For example, I love Krispy Kreme donuts. I know that I should not eat too many of them for health reasons. If my friends and I drive by a Krispy Kreme donut shop and the *"Hot Now"* sign is on, then I must actively resist the temptation to stop. Nobody can eat just one, right? It is difficult.

If I confess to my friends that Krispy Kreme donuts is a weakness in my foundation and I really do not need to eat them for health reasons, then my friends can help me avoid the sign that brings temptation. Therefore, I am avoiding the temptation instead of resisting the temptation.

By confessing a fault, I avoid a fall. This makes life much easier.

CHAPTER 8

FASTING AWAY HUNGER

FASTING AWAY HUNGER

God never invites His children to get hungry. God's invitation is to feast. In fact, God commanded His people to feast seven different times in a year, but required a fast only once; *on the Day of Atonement*. So what is the deal with fasting?

The terms "fast" or "fasting" occur several times in Scripture. A fast typically involves abstaining from food, and may also involve abstaining from drink. Sometimes it involves only partial abstinence from certain foods. Fasts could be for a single meal, a single day, or even up to forty days at a time.

In a world dominated by fast-food temples and golden arches, fasting seems out of place and even out of step with our culture and present reality. In fact, many churches no longer even talk about the subject of fasting. I believe the reason for this is because fasting is often abused to create a false sense of spirituality. People love to show off their discipline and religiousness.

Jesus warned of this hypocrisy through fasting:

> [16] Moreover, when ye fast, be not, as the hypocrites, of a sad countenance: for they disfigure their faces, that they may appear unto men to fast.
> Verily I say unto you, they have their reward.
>
> [17] But thou, when thou fastest, anoint thy head, and wash thy face;
>
> [18] that thou appear not unto men to fast but unto thy Father which is in secret: and thy Father, which seeth in secret, shall reward thee openly.
> **Matthew 6:16-18**

So even according to Jesus, fasting *does* have a benefit. It also comes with a reward. What is the reward?

FEEDING THE HUNGRY SOUL

Many people sincerely try to fast and end up further away from the Lord than when they began. I have numerous books in my office on the topic of fasting, many of them written by influential believers. Sadly, in my research, very few have God's complete definition of what a true fast actually *is*.

God gives us His expectation for true fasting:

> [1] Cry aloud, spare not,
> lift up thy voice like a trumpet,
> and shew my people their transgression,
> and the house of Jacob their sins.
>
> [2] Yet they seek me daily,
> and delight to know my ways,
> as a nation that did righteousness,
> and forsook not the ordinance of their God:
> they ask of me the ordinances of justice;
> they take delight in approaching to God.
>
> [3] Wherefore have we fasted,
> say they, and thou seest not?
> wherefore have we afflicted our soul,
> and thou takest no knowledge?
> Behold, in the day of your fast ye find pleasure,
> and exact all your labours.
>
> [4] Behold, ye fast for strife and debate,
> and to smite with the fist of wickedness:
> ye shall not fast as ye do this day,
> to make your voice to be heard on high.
>
> [5] Is it such a fast that I have chosen?
> a day for a man to afflict his soul?
> is it to bow down his head as a bulrush,
> and to spread sackcloth and ashes under him?
> wilt thou call this a fast,
> and an acceptable day to the Lord?

FASTING AWAY HUNGER

⁶ Is not this the fast that I have chosen?
to loose the bands of wickedness,
to undo the heavy burdens,
and to let the oppressed go free,
and that ye break every yoke?

⁷ Is it not to deal thy bread to the hungry,
and that thou bring the poor that are cast out to thy house?
when thou seest the naked, that thou cover him;
and that thou hide not thyself from thine own flesh?

⁸ Then shall thy light break forth as the morning,
 and thine health shall spring forth speedily:
and thy righteousness shall go before thee;
the glory of the Lord shall be thy reward.

⁹ Then shalt thou call, and the Lord shall answer;
thou shalt cry, and he shall say, Here I am.
If thou take away from the midst of thee the yoke,
 the putting forth of the finger, and speaking vanity;

¹⁰ And if thou draw out thy soul to the hungry,
and satisfy the afflicted soul;
then shall thy light rise in obscurity,
and thy darkness be as the noon day:

¹¹ And the Lord shall guide thee continually,
and satisfy thy soul in drought, and make fat thy bones:
and thou shalt be like a watered garden,
and like a spring of water, whose waters fail not.

¹² And they that shall be of thee shall build the old waste places:
 thou shalt raise up the foundations of many generations;
and thou shalt be called, The repairer of the breach,
The restorer of paths to dwell in.

> ¹³ If thou turn away thy foot from the sabbath,
> from doing thy pleasure on my holy day;
> and call the sabbath a delight, the holy of the Lord, honourable;
> and shalt honour him, not doing thine own ways,
> nor finding thine own pleasure,
> nor speaking thine own words:
>
> ¹⁴ Then shalt thou delight thyself in the Lord;
> and I will cause thee to ride upon the high places of the earth,
> and feed thee with the heritage of Jacob thy father:
> for the mouth of the Lord hath spoken it.
> **Isaiah 58:1-14**

In verse 5, God rebukes His people about the way in which they were fasting. In the next verse God says: *"Is this not the fast that I have chosen?"* God explains to His people exactly what He expects when they fast. Without meeting the expectations that God has given us concerning fasting, how can we expect our efforts to please Him?

Fasting should never be a burden. It should never be oppressive. It should never be a yoke. God says that a true fast will loose the bands of wickedness, undo heavy burdens, let the oppressed go free, and break every yoke.

God says that a true fast is not simply *giving up* our food, but a true fast is when we *give away* our food. Fasting God's way is inviting the poor to a meal at your expense.

It seems crazy to me now, but there was a time in my youthfulness that I selfishly thought I would even save some money by not eating all week. It's not about saving money. It's not about losing weight. Fasting God's way is ordering that cheeseburger and giving it away. Take it to the homeless child on the street and feed those who are considered the least among society. Minister grace into ***their lives.***

FASTING AWAY HUNGER

By the way, Jesus said:

> [35] For I was an hungred, and ye gave me meat:
> I was thirsty, and ye gave me drink:
> I was a stranger, and ye took me in:
>
> [36] Naked, and ye clothed me:
> I was sick, and ye visited me:
> I was in prison, and ye came unto me.
>
> [37] Then shall the righteous answer him, saying,
> Lord, when saw we thee an hungred, and fed thee?
> or thirsty, and gave thee drink?
>
> [38] When saw we thee a stranger, and took thee in?
> or naked, and clothed thee?
>
> [39] Or when saw we thee sick, or in prison,
> and came unto thee?
>
> [40] And the King shall answer and say unto them,
> Verily I say unto you, Inasmuch as ye have done it
> unto one of the least of these my brethren,
> ye have done it unto me.
> **Matthew 25:35-40**

This is remarkable. Jesus says that the least important person who is hungry, the least important person who is thirsty, the least important person of the naked, the least important person among the sick, the least important in prison, and the least important stranger should be treated as if we were caring for Jesus Christ Himself.

This is what a true fast is all about and God promises a reward for so doing. He says in Isaiah 58, that light will break forth as the morning. He says our health shall spring forth and the glory of the Lord shall be our reward.

FEEDING THE HUNGRY SOUL

When we are full of His glory, we shall call and He will answer. When we cry, God will say *Here I am.* That is a promise! This is why Jesus told His disciples, *"this kind goeth not out but by prayer and fasting"* (Matthew 17:21).

God promised to those who keep His true fast that He will satisfy their soul in the drought and make *fat* their bones. If we fast like this, God says we will be as a watered garden, full of His Spirit, with no place for the Devil or his trash.

Fasting—true fasting—is about delighting ourselves in the Lord by caring for those around us, seeking the lost, and helping the needy. Fasting is truly not about starvation. Fasting is about *feeding others* and being fed by *Jesus* in return. **Fasting is about destroying hunger.**

CHAPTER 9

THE FRUIT *of* THE SPIRIT

THE FRUIT OF THE SPIRIT

The fruit of the Spirit is a well-known phrase among believers, but it is seldom part of our spiritual diet. In this chapter, let us pause to consider what the fruit of the Spirit *is* (and *is not*) and how well it is received in our lives.

[16] This I say then, Walk in the Spirit,
and ye shall not fulfil the lust of the flesh.

[17] For the flesh lusteth against the Spirit,
and the Spirit against the flesh:
and these are contrary the one to the other:
so that ye cannot do the things that ye would.

[18] But if ye be led of the Spirit,
ye are not under the law.

[19] Now the works of the flesh are manifest, which are these;
Adultery, fornication, uncleanness, lasciviousness,

[20] Idolatry, witchcraft, hatred, variance,
emulations, wrath, strife, seditions, heresies,

[21] Envyings, murders, drunkenness, revellings, and such like:
of the which I tell you before,
as I have also told you in time past,
that they which do such things
shall not inherit the kingdom of God.

[22] But the fruit of the Spirit is love, joy, peace,
longsuffering, gentleness, goodness, faith,

[23] Meekness, temperance:
against such there is no law.

[24] And they that are Christ's have crucified the flesh
with the affections and lusts.

[25] If we live in the Spirit,
let us also walk in the Spirit.

[26] Let us not be desirous of vain glory,
provoking one another, envying one another.
Galatians 5:16-26

Notice that the works of the flesh are not fruit. These works are *manifestations* of our corrupt flesh. When we fail to indulge and be filled with the Spirit, we will manifest the corruption of our flesh through adultery, fornication, uncleanness, and other fleshly manifestations.

Do not be deceived...these works are not a contrast between the unsaved and the saved. Even the believer still has a body of flesh that is at war with his spirit. If a believer fails to be filled with the Spirit, they will have a void—a hunger, a lust—and may seek to fill that void. As stated before, if Satan cannot fill your void with bad things, he will put good things there. His primary concern is not what goes in the void. He just wants the void to remain.

This is why James 4:3 tells us that believers sometimes pray for things to consume on their own lusts. Prayer is not evil, neither is God's answer to prayer. Yet James says that if we are not careful, we can ask amiss to consume on our own lusts. We sometimes even petition God for things that we think will satisfy our void rather than being filled with the Spirit.

The real answer to satisfy our void is complying with God's simple command to *"be filled with the Spirit."* He does not say, **being** filled, but rather **be** filled. You should be full right now. You ought always to **be** filled. Otherwise, Satan will always take full advantage of the void.

How does the fruit of the Spirit impact the lives of those who are united with Christ? To begin with, the fruit of the Spirit cannot be produced by us. It is not the fruit of the believer; it is the fruit of the Spirit. It is not a system of self-improvement. People have a lot of

THE FRUIT OF THE SPIRIT

ideas on how to make the *inner you* stronger and better. Just Google *"self help"* and you will find thousands of books claiming to improve your inner self. This might be Oprah Winfrey and the Dalai Lama's market, but it is no place for believers.

The fruit of the Spirit is cultivated by God for us. Remember the picture of childbirth we discussed in a previous chapter. Work and travail are marks of the curse, not the marks of an abundant life. We were designed to rest in Christ as the infant rests in the womb. We are to abide in Him and receive from Him all that we need. We do not have to work to be filled with the Spirit. We must rest in Christ.

Ever since Adam lost his position in the garden where he literally dwelt in the presence of God, God's mission has been to reconcile man back into His presence through salvation, redemption, and restoration. He wants us back in Him.

SPIRITUAL INSULATION

Let me ask you a question:
Is sin internal or external?

Are pride and lust internal or external? For example, one man may see a woman scantily dressed and think nothing of it. At the same time, another man sees her and has trouble controlling his thoughts. We may treat temptation as a matter of merely removing ourselves from its presence. That should always be our first choice, but that is not always possible. Temptations will rise, sometimes when we least expect it.

The secret to victory over sin is not external.

Of course, as the world waxes worse and worse, the external temptations will as well. I believe it is best to avoid as much unnecessary temptation as possible, but how we deal with temptation is an internal matter. Nothing external can *make* us sin.

If I see something sinful, it cannot make me sin. If it could, the burden of guilt would be on that thing, and God could be accused of allowing us to be forced to sin. Yet God does not tempt man to sin, much less make him sin.

It is the void within us that causes temptation. Unless the void is destroyed, Satan will always have a place to work in our life, "giving place to the devil" (Ephesians 4:27). You and I will always have a yearning and we will be tempted to satisfy that yearning with sin.

Believers often isolate themselves from things as if isolation will keep them from sin. *Do not go here, do not have that;* those places and things cannot make us sin. **Isolation simply creates a weak spiritual immune system.**

People sometimes mistake isolation for victory, when really, it is a self-made prison. Unfortunately, it is often difficult to get someone out of a prison cell that they have already begun to decorate. Isolationist believers may appear to have high morals, but they end up in bondage that is unnecessary. If you *insulate* a believer with the fruit of the Spirit there is no need to *isolate* the believer. Jesus was not isolated from sinners, but insulated by the Spirit as He walked among the sinners. *It is not isolation we need from the world; it is insulation we need by the Spirit as we live in the world.*

As you consider the fruit of the Spirit in your life, allow Scripture to guide you and examine your heart. Give your life a spiritual checkup. Learning more about the fruit of the Spirit is a challenge to our direction. Understanding more about the fruit of the Spirit will inspire and encourage us to trust God's promise that He will never leave us hungry.

THE FRUIT OF THE SPIRIT

> I have been young, and now am old;
> yet have I not seen the righteous forsaken,
> nor his seed begging bread.
> **Psalm 37:25**

The fruit of the Spirit is a study in practical Godliness. It reminds us that faithful, Christ-centered living is demonstrated by how full we are with God.

IS YOUR CUP RUNNING OVER?

Many believers are caught daily on the treadmill of gritting their teeth to do God's will. Such attempts to conquer our rebellion or sin will leave us exhausted every time. The way to obtain victory is to flood our minds with God's thoughts by feasting on the fruit of the Spirit.

Notice that it does *not* say, "the fruit *from* the Spirit." It says: "the fruit *of* the Spirit." We *do not produce* the fruit of the Spirit, but we get to enjoy the fruit. It is not my fruit; it is the Holy Spirit's fruit, and I am commanded to be filled.

*I am **commanded** to be filled with the Spirit's **love**.*

*I am **commanded** to be filled with the Spirit's **joy**.*

*I am **commanded** to be filled with the Spirit's **peace**.*

*I am **commanded** to be filled with the Spirit's **longsuffering**.*

*I am **commanded** to be filled with the Spirit's **gentleness**.*

*I am **commanded** to be filled with the Spirit's **goodness**.*

*I am **commanded** to be filled with the Spirit's **faith**.*

*I am **commanded** to be filled with the Spirit's **meekness**.*

*I am **commanded** to be filled with the Spirit's **temperance**.*

There is no law which forbids me from indulging on this fruit. It is God's *all you can eat buffet*.

Adam was commanded to eat freely and indulge on the fruit of the garden. Likewise, we are commanded to indulge on the fruit of the Spirit and be filled.

WALK IN THE SPIRIT

Galatians 5:25 says *"If we live in the Spirit, let us also walk in the Spirit."* **Don't miss this:** it is possible to be *alive* in the Spirit without *walking* in the Spirit.

For example, in **1 Corinthians 3:1** a baby believer is likened to a carnally-minded man; *"And I, brethren, could not speak unto you as unto **spiritual**, but as unto **carnal**, even as unto babes in Christ."*

A person in Christ has been regenerated. Their dead spirit has been quickened by the Spirit of God. We call this salvation. Once in Christ, we soon find our need for the fruit of the Spirit. This is where we begin to walk in the Spirit.

Children are not born walking. They have to grow, to learn, they fall and then have to get back up. They keep eating, growing, falling and getting back up. And eating, and eating, and eating, growing, falling, getting back up. That is how a child learns to walk.

It is the fruit of the Spirit which helps us grow.
It is the fruit of the Spirit which strengthens our walk.
It is the fruit of the Spirit which sustains and satisfies our soul.
So eat. Be filled.

This is such an important truth because we were created with these needs and God gives us a way to be satisfied.

THE FRUIT OF THE SPIRIT

I was born with a need for love, joy, peace, longsuffering, gentleness, goodness, faith, meekness, and temperance.

This is precisely why the world so hungrily searches for these things.

*They are starving for **love**.*

*They are starving for **joy**.*

*They are starving for **peace**.*

*They are starving for **longsuffering**.*

*They are starving for **gentleness**.*

*They are starving for **goodness**.*

*They are starving for **faith**.*

*They are starving for **meekness**.*

*They are starving for **temperance**.*

Every person was born with each of these needs. Unfortunately, too many people pursue the elements of the fruit while denying the source of that fruit. They want the gift, but not the Gift Giver. Satisfaction from their hunger can be found only in Him.

The believer is not immune to this vain struggle. Christian's may also seek to fill the voids in their life with something other than the fruit God has offered them, but that leads to sin. We must pursue the Spirit and not the things of the world. Be filled with the Spirit; He will fill us up and destroy the void.

Notice that the fruit is not plural, but singular. It is not the "fruits of the Spirit," but the "fruit of the Spirit."

*This is important to understand in our daily walk, for it means that if I need **love**, I do not seek after love, but I seek the Spirit.*

*If I need **joy**, I do not seek joy, but I seek the Spirit.*

*If I need **peace**, I do not seek peace, but I seek the Spirit.*

*If I need **longsuffering**, I do not seek longsuffering, but I seek the Spirit.*

*If I need **gentleness**, I do not seek gentleness, but I seek the Spirit.*

*If I need **goodness**, I do not seek goodness, but I seek the Spirit.*

*If I need **faith**, I do not seek faith, but I seek the Spirit.*

*If I need **meekness**, I do not seek meekness, but I seek the Spirit.*

*If I need **temperance**, I do not seek temperance, but I seek the Spirit.*

When I am full of the Spirit, His fruit will satisfy my every longing. Be filled!

TEMPERANCE IS NOT SELF CONTROL

Many Christians who struggle with temptations soon realize they are not able to control themselves. Thus, focusing on "self-control" is futile and it is also a work of the flesh.

"Self-control" given by the Spirit is inherently contradictory. It is an oxymoron to use self and Spirit as one; if it is of self, it is not of the Spirit. The word "temperance" is an accurate translation because that word does not focus on self. What we need instead of *self* control is *Spirit* control.

Temperance is the Spirit's strength over self. It is not self-control, but Christ-control. To indulge on Spiritual temperance is to enjoy every physical pleasure in moderation.

In the Olympics, the best athletes are under the control of their coaches in all things. The same goes for the good soldier who submits to authority. It is important for the athlete in competition and it is important for soldiers in winning the war. It should be the same for Christians, if we want to finish the race and win our crowns.

THE FRUIT OF THE SPIRIT

Being accountable and placing yourself under the control of another person may be a little safer in some areas, but it is still not sufficient to glorify God. Bringing self under Jesus Christ is the only way to enjoy fullness in Him and win over the addictions and powers that have controlled you. That is temperance.

ABIDING IN CHRIST

Walking in the Spirit also means that personal priority lists disappear. We often shape our identity around that which we crave the most. The possibility of losing (not to mention voluntarily forfeiting) that identity brings massive fear. What do you fear most about letting go? Is it a relationship, your family, security, success, a dream, your children, money, or what about life itself?

What did Christ say?

> If any man come to me,
> and hate not his father, and mother,
> and wife, and children,
> and brethren, and sisters,
> yea, and his own life also,
> he cannot be my disciple.
> **Luke 14:25**

Those words either comfort you or terrify you. Which is it?

The truth is—when I abide in Christ, then I can love my father, mother, brother, sister, and even myself *in* Christ.

I have heard some people say that "outside of Christ, my spouse is my best friend." Please do not misunderstand, I know what they mean by that comment, but according to Scripture nothing should be *outside of Christ*. He is my *only* priority. I love my wife *in* Christ, I love my children *in* Christ, I love my church *in* Christ.

FEEDING THE HUNGRY SOUL

Walking in the Spirit and feasting on His fruit will give us perfect satisfaction and contentment. This is not some philosophical theory that sounds good on paper; it is a reality in the life of every believer who has learned to indulge and be filled.

God's Word says: *"Godliness with contentment is great gain"* (1 Timothy 6:6). Resting in Christ makes me godly. Feasting on the fruit of the Spirit makes me content. Contentment is not a settlement, but a satisfaction. It is not to pacify, but to please. It is not the adjustment of an attitude, but the filling of the Spirit. It is peace, it is tranquility, it is fullness, it is rest.

So how do we feast on this fruit?

> [1] Blessed is the man that walketh not
> in the counsel of the ungodly,
> nor standeth in the way of sinners,
> nor sitteth in the seat of the scornful.
>
> [2] But his delight is in the law of the Lord;
> and in his law doth he meditate day and night.
>
> [3] And he shall be like a tree planted by the rivers of water,
> that bringeth forth his fruit in his season;
> his leaf also shall not wither;
> and whatsoever he doeth shall prosper.
> **Psalm 1:1-3**

The man who desires to prosper and be filled must meditate on the Word both day and night. Jesus said:

> It is the spirit that quickeneth;
> the flesh profiteth nothing:
> the words that I speak unto you,
> they are spirit, and they are life.
> **John 6:63**

Literally, the words of Christ are Spirit.

THE FRUIT OF THE SPIRIT

Do not allegorize a plain truth; believe it and live it. Do you want to follow the Spirit? Follow the words of Christ. Do you want to be filled with the Spirit? Fill your heart with the words of Christ.

> Thy words were found, and I did eat them;
> and thy word was unto me the joy and rejoicing of mine heart:
> for I am called by thy name, O Lord God of hosts.
> **Jeremiah 15:16**

Following is a sample list of individuals in Scripture who were feasting on the different elements of the Spirit's fruit.

The Apostle John said:

> And from Jesus Christ, who is the faithful witness,
> and the first begotten of the dead,
> and the prince of the kings of the earth.
> Unto him that **loved** us,
> and washed us from our sins in his own blood.
> **Revelation 1:5**

The Apostle Paul said:

> And not only so,
> but we also **joy** in God through our Lord Jesus Christ,
> by whom we have now received the atonement.
> **Romans 5:8**

> And the **peace** of God, which passeth all understanding, shall keep your hearts and minds through Christ Jesus.
> **Philippians 4:7**

> And be found in him,
> not having mine own righteousness, which is of the law,
> but that which is through the **faith** of Christ,
> the righteousness which is of God by faith:
> **Philippians 3:8-9**

FEEDING THE HUNGRY SOUL

Moses tells us:

> And the LORD passed by before him, and proclaimed,
> The LORD, The LORD God, merciful and gracious,
> **longsuffering**, and abundant in goodness and truth
> **Exodus 34:6**

King David said:

> Thou hast also given me the shield of thy salvation: and thy **gentleness** hath made me great.
> **2 Samuel 22:36**

> Remember not the sins of my youth, nor my transgressions: according to thy mercy remember thou me for thy **goodness'** sake, O LORD.
> **Psalm.25:7**

The Apostle Peter said:

> 4 Whereby are given unto us
> exceeding great and precious promises:
> that by these ye might be partakers of the divine nature,
> having escaped the corruption that is in the world through lust.

> 5 And beside this, giving all diligence,
> add to your faith virtue;
> and to virtue knowledge;

> 6 And to knowledge **temperance**;
> and to temperance patience;
> and to patience godliness;

> 7 And to godliness brotherly kindness;
> and to brotherly kindness charity.

> 8 For if these things be in you, and abound,
> they make you that ye shall neither be barren nor unfruitful
> in the knowledge of our Lord Jesus Christ.
> **2 Peter 1:4-8**

THE FRUIT OF THE SPIRIT

Like Adam, we should never forget that God has freely given us fruit to consume. We can indulge and be filled with as much as we want and *against such there is no law.* In fact, we are **commanded** to do it. We were created to indulge on this fruit.

But also like Adam, ***if we fail to freely eat and be filled*** with the fruit God gives us, ***we tempt ourselves.***

> The full soul loatheth an honeycomb;
> but to the hungry soul, every bitter thing is sweet.
> **Proverbs 27:7**

You will not desire anything more when you are full, no matter how sweet and tempting it may be, including the sweetest honeycomb. However, if you fail to indulge on the fruit of the Spirit, your hunger will tempt you to consume anything you can get, including the bitter substitutes of Satan.

Examine yourself... are you filled?

CHAPTER 10

FEASTING AWAY FEAR

FEASTING AWAY FEAR

Life can be risky and difficult. It is filled with opportunities and reasons for fear and anxiety. I am referring to all levels of fear, from general apprehension and worry, to dread and terror.

Fear normally starts out when we are very young. There are fears of things like darkness, monsters, etc. We may experience fears in our teenage years of things like rejection, humiliation and failure. Adulthood is also filled with possible fears such as the fear of disease, death, financial problems, broken relationships, loved ones being hurt, storms, failure, aging, crime, etc. Everyone knows what it is like to be filled with fear and anxiety.

We are an anxiety-laden society. Just look at the sales of books dealing with fear and anxiety and the use of drugs needed to calm people down.

Fear is very unpleasant and it is very harmful physically, mentally, and even spiritually; for as the Scriptures tell us in Matthew 13:22, fear or anxiety chokes out the word of God. For this reason, fear can be very displeasing and dishonoring to God.

We all want solutions to the problem of fear. We all want answers to eliminate anxiety. We are looking for something to relieve us from our fears, something to reassure us. We're looking for some source of security that will instill a perfect confidence and peace within our hearts.

Some people look for that security in their bank account. Some seek that reassurance in a relationship. Others have placed their trust in the government, the latest drugs, and so on. None of these are real solutions because none of them offer total security or absolute reassurance. No amount of money, success, or any position in life can truly give you peace in every situation. So the question becomes; ***How can we have victory over fear?***

The answer to this important question is given in 1 John 4:18: "There is no fear in love; but perfect love casteth out fear: because fear hath torment. He that feareth is not made perfect in love."

Subtract love and you lose courage—you lost heart. Courage is a product of love. A mother will jump into a cage of rattlesnakes to save her baby, not because she is immune to snake venom, but because she loves her child. Love is the great difference between courage and stupidity. Since courage is a product of love, any act of bravery that is not motivated by love is lunacy. Christ went to the cross, despising the shame; but for the joy that was set before Him, He chose to march forward. In other words, it was His love that gave Him the courage to press on.

How do we feast on this perfect love?

PERFECT LOVE

[15] Whosoever shall confess that Jesus is the Son of God, God dwelleth in him, and he in God.

[16] And we have known and believed
the love that God hath to us. God is love;
and he that dwelleth in love dwelleth in God,
and God in him.

[17] Herein is our love made perfect,
that we may have boldness in the day of judgment:
because as he is, so are we in this world.

[18] There is no fear in love;
but perfect love casteth out fear:
because fear hath torment.
He that feareth is not made perfect in love.

[19] We love him, because he first loved us.

FEASTING AWAY FEAR

> [20] If a man say, I love God, and hateth his brother, he is a liar:
> for he that loveth not his brother whom he hath seen,
> how can he love God whom he hath not seen?
>
> [21] And this commandment have we from him,
> That he who loveth God love his brother also.
> **1 John 4:15-21**

> But whoso keepeth his word,
> in him verily is the love of God perfected:
> hereby know we that we are in him.
> **1 John 2:5**

In the Old Testament, we are commanded to love God and others. This is scriptural law, but they are also called the Great Commandments. Did you know there's a commandment even greater than those two commandments?

Remember the lawyer who approached Jesus and asked Him what was the greatest commandment *in the Law?* Jesus responded with these words:

> 37 Jesus said unto him,
> Thou shalt love the Lord thy God with all thy heart,
> and with all thy soul, and with all thy mind.
>
> 38 This is the first and great commandment.
>
> 39 And the second is like unto it,
> Thou shalt love thy neighbour as thyself.
>
> 40 On these two commandments
> hang all the law and the prophets.
> **Matthew 22:37-40**

Notice carefully that Jesus did NOT say, "This is *my* rule for you." He was simply summarizing the Old Testament Law, which we see by His statement: *"On these two commandments hang all the law and the prophets."*

FEEDING THE HUNGRY SOUL

Once we understand that, we can then make sense of the new commandment:

> 34 A new commandment I give unto you,
> That ye love one another; **as I have loved you**,
> that ye also love one another.
>
> 35 By this shall all men know that ye are my disciples,
> if ye have love one to another.
> **John 13:34-35**

During His earthly ministry, Jesus did not command us to love our neighbor as ourselves. That was a command in the Mosaic Law. Rather, Jesus commanded us to love others as He loves us.

The bar has been raised.

The Mosaic Law commanded you to love God and to love your neighbor, but Jesus is saying that He wants you to *love all others in the same way that He loves you.*

This is perfect love.
This is unconditional love.
This is sacrificial love.
This is the type of love that does not seek its own.
This is Christ's standard. This is the command to follow.

What is higher than my love for a neighbor or even my love for God? It is Christ's love for me. That is how I am to love others.

Feeding your pain creates fear. Feeding your pleasure creates addiction. Feasting on the fruit of the Spirit brings peace.

FEASTING AWAY FEAR

> Thou wilt keep him in **perfect peace,**
> **whose mind is stayed on thee:**
> because he trusteth in thee.
> **Isaiah 26:3**

Jesus is that perfect love which casts out all fear. The believer has no worries when resting on the soft pillow of God's sovereignty. While there may be thousands of pills that can give you sleep, they have yet to make a pill that can give you rest. Nevertheless, Jesus said: *"Come unto me, all ye that labour, and are heavy laden, and I will give you rest."* That is love.

Now, consume His love.

> Fear thou not; for I am with thee:
> be not dismayed; for I am thy God:
> I will strengthen thee; yea, I will help thee; yea,
> I will uphold thee with the right hand of my righteousness.
> **Isaiah 41:10**

FEEDING THE HUNGRY SOUL

CHAPTER 11

FEASTING FOR TODAY

FEASTING FOR TODAY

Think about how physical hunger affects you. Your body is forced to compensate for inadequate nutrition by curbing physical and mental activity. Hunger deprives you of your initiative and ability to concentrate. It leaves you in a state of apathy. When your body is starved, your immune system is weakened and you become more vulnerable to infectious disease.

Do you realize the same kind of thing could happen to your soul when you fail to feed on God's Word? Did you get that? ***Do you realize the same kind of thing could happen to your soul when you fail to feed on God's Word?***

Spiritual hunger curbs your spiritual activity, energy, and focus. It makes you apathetic and weakens your spiritual immune system, making you much more vulnerable to temptation.

We must regularly feed on God's Word to remain spiritually healthy. We must continually and purposefully nurture our spirit with the Word of God.

> As newborn babes, desire the sincere milk of the word,
> that ye may grow thereby.
> 1 Peter 2:2

> Neither have I gone back
> from the commandment of his lips;
> I have esteemed the words of his mouth
> more than my necessary food.
> **Job 23:12**

DAY BY DAY

[9] After this manner therefore pray ye: Our Father which art in heaven, Hallowed be thy name.

[10] Thy kingdom come, Thy will be done in earth, as it is in heaven.

[11] Give us this day our daily bread.

[12] And forgive us our debts, as we forgive our debtors.

[13] And lead us not into temptation, but deliver us from evil: For thine is the kingdom, and the power, and the glory, for ever. Amen.
Matthew 6:9-13

Notice verse 11: "Give us this day our daily bread."

Obviously Jesus was not telling His disciples to pray only for bread, but bread was a staple in the diet of the Jews. Furthermore, bread was a powerful symbol of God's provision for His people in the Old Testament. Remember how God cared for the Israelites when they were in the wilderness after their exodus from Egypt? Life in the wilderness was so hard the people began to complain that it would be better to be back in Egypt. At least in Egypt, they had plenty of food. God responded to Moses by promising to "rain bread from heaven" (**Exodus 16:4**).

The next morning when the dew lifted they discovered thin flakes covering the ground, as fine as frost and tasting like honey. In my imagination, all I see is Krispy Kreme donuts. In any case, God miraculously fed His people from heaven by giving them bread.

The bread was a symbol of Jesus Christ. He referred to Himself as the Bread of Life. We must continually feast on this Spiritual bread. We must be filled with Him.

How is this possible?

Jesus is the Word (John 1). Ask yourself this question, would you rather spend an evening with Jesus Christ in person or read the Word of God? On the evening of His arrest, Jesus comforted His disciples by saying: "Nevertheless I tell you the truth; **It is expedient for you that I go away**: for if I go not away, the

FEASTING FOR TODAY

Comforter will not come unto you; but if I depart, I will send him unto you." (John 16:7)

What does expedient mean? It means beneficial. Jesus was talking about the Holy Spirit that would lead and guide them into all truth, using them to give us the written Word.

Jesus deemed the Spirit's presence within us to be more beneficial than His physical presence, yet we crave the physical and neglect the Spirit. We should be feasting on the Bread of Life every single day. We should be asking for this Spiritual Bread day by day.

Remember the following as you pray each day:

1. Praying for daily bread does not cultivate a spirit of "taking" but a spirit of "receiving." We cannot take from God what He does not give. It would not be a gift if we were able to take it. He gives us our daily bread. We must be prepared to receive it.

2. God desires to replenish us. Throughout Scripture we find that God loves to replenish. Charles Spurgeon once said: "We quickly lose the nourishment and strength of yesterday's bread. We must feed our souls daily upon the manna God has given us."

3. Daily bread is always fresh. Think about it...our need for daily bread does not require our effort; God supplies our need every day. It's up to Him. When He meets my need day by day, I learn to rely on the Gift-Giver rather than the gift!

4. Daily bread from God means tomorrow's bread is certain. I can trust to be fed tomorrow because He is trustworthy. This means that I can fill up today and I can eat my fill today because my hope is not in the bread, but in the Bread-Maker.

OUR NEED FOR HOPE

We desperately need hope. People are spiritually sick without hope in God. God's Word states: *"Hope deferred maketh the heart sick: but when the desire cometh, it is a tree of life."* (**Proverbs 13:12**)

Hope is to our soul what energy is to our bodies. Hope is the spiritual energy generated in the soul when we believe that our future is good, even when our present reality is bad. Our souls must have hope to keep going, just as our bodies must have energy to keep going.

Hope is something we feel only about the future, whether it is ten minutes or ten thousand years from now. We're never hopeful about the past. We can be grateful for the past. The past may inspire or even guarantee a hopeful future for us, but all the wonderful things that have happened to us in the past will not fuel our hope if our future looks bleak. We must have hope—that Blessed Hope—every day to keep going.

So, even if you have filled up today, thoroughly feasted on the fruit of the Spirit today, allowed God to totally destroy every void in your life today, you must never forget to eat again tomorrow! You must feast again and again—day by day.

CHAPTER 12

FEASTING ON FORGIVENESS

FEASTING ON FORGIVENESS

Trusting in fallible humans can leave the heart in pieces. We are left with broken trust, hurt feelings, and damaged relationships. We can even fail to meet the standards and goals that we set for ourselves.

Forgiveness is commanded throughout the Scriptures, but sometimes it just seems so hard to produce. Forgiving others can be a huge challenge and forgiving ourselves can sometimes seem impossible.

So how can we learn to forgive? Let's look at a few truths that will help us.

It is important to understand that God never commanded you to trust people. God commanded you to love people and trust Him. Know the difference, because your joy can depend on it.

Other people can betray your trust and let you down, but God will never let you down. Trusting Him *above* all others allows your joy to be as consistent as God's character.

Spiritual judgment discerns the intent of the heart behind an action. While I cannot know your true intentions, God certainly does. I cannot judge anyone after this fashion, but I can trust God to execute judgment and bring justice on my behalf. Therefore, no matter what happens, my trust in God provides the foundation for extending forgiveness as I am commanded. I must always forgive, even if someone does not deserve my forgiveness; Christ always deserves my obedience.

I did not say that it would always be easy, but we can cultivate a heart of forgiveness for all of the wrongs done against us? Let's see what the Scriptures say.

FEEDING THE HUNGRY SOUL

In Matthew 18 we find the well known passage where Peter asks Jesus about forgiveness. The ensuing conversation was not a public lesson, but a teachable moment between Jesus and Peter:

> [21] Then came Peter to him, and said,
> Lord, how oft shall my brother sin against me,
> and I forgive him? till seven times?
>
> [22] Jesus saith unto him,
> I say not unto thee, Until seven times:
> but, Until seventy times seven.
>
> [23] Therefore is the kingdom of heaven
> likened unto a certain king,
> which would take account of his servants.
>
> [24] And when he had begun to reckon,
> one was brought unto him,
> which owed him ten thousand talents.
>
> [25] But forasmuch as he had not to pay,
> his lord commanded him to be sold,
> and his wife, and children, and all that he had,
> and payment to be made.
>
> [26] The servant therefore fell down,
> and worshipped him, saying,
> Lord, have patience with me, and I will pay thee all.
>
> [27] Then the lord of that servant was moved with compassion,
> and loosed him, and forgave him the debt.
>
> [28] But the same servant went out,
> and found one of his fellowservants,
> which owed him an hundred pence:
> and he laid hands on him,
> and took him by the throat, saying,
> Pay me that thou owest.

FEASTING ON FORGIVENESS

²⁹ And his fellowservant fell down at his feet,
and besought him, saying,
Have patience with me, and I will pay thee all.

³⁰ And he would not:
but went and cast him into prison,
till he should pay the debt.

³¹ So when his fellowservants saw what was done,
they were very sorry,
 and came and told unto their lord
all that was done.

³² Then his lord, after that he had called him,
said unto him, O thou wicked servant,
I forgave thee all that debt, because thou desiredst me:

³³ Shouldest not thou also have had compassion
on thy fellowservant, even as I had pity on thee?

³⁴ And his lord was wroth,
and delivered him to the tormentors,
till he should pay all that was due unto him.

³⁵ So likewise shall my heavenly Father do also unto you,
if ye from your hearts forgive not
every one his brother their trespasses.
Matthew 18:21-35

Notice the servant had nothing to offer in exchange for forgiveness. He had no money to repay the debt, so he dropped to his knees and appealed to the master's compassion. And it worked. The king was moved with compassion and forgave the servant of his enormous debt.

There were no conditions applied.
There were no bargains made.
There were no arguments offered.
The servant pleaded and the king forgave him.

That is a picture of what Christ did for us. We had a debt we could not pay. We had no bargaining chips and no argument to stand on. Yet Christ died to afford us forgiveness.

> [11] For the grace of God that bringeth salvation
> hath appeared to **all men,**
>
> [12] Teaching us that,
> denying ungodliness and worldly lusts,
> we should live soberly, righteously, and godly,
> in this present world;
>
> [13] Looking for that blessed hope,
> and the glorious appearing of the great God
> and our Saviour Jesus Christ;
>
> [14] Who gave himself for us,
> that **he might redeem us from all iniquity,**
> and purify unto himself a peculiar people,
> zealous of good works.
>
> [15] These things speak, and exhort,
> and rebuke **with all authority.**
> Let no man despise thee.
> **Titus 2:11-15**

If the grace of God that brings salvation has appeared unto all men, then it has appeared even to the worst of men. God's grace appeared to every genocidal dictator, every heartless murderer, every serial rapist, and every fornicator who ever lived. That grace appeared on Calvary, and it abounds greater than all iniquity.

"But where sin abounded, grace did much more abound." No matter the sin you may have committed, Jesus gave Himself for you that He might redeem you from all iniquity. There is not one iniquity from which you cannot be redeemed.

Think about that. For therein is our standard of forgiveness. The king said: *"I forgave thee **all** that debt, **because thou desiredst me**: Shouldest not thou also have had compassion on thy fellowservant, **even as I had pity on thee?**"*

We have nothing to offer, yet Christ offered us forgiveness because we desired it of Him. Should we not go and do likewise?

FOCUS ON GOD'S FORGIVENESS

Remember that Peter and Jesus most likely had this conversation one-on-one. Just a short time later Peter denied the Master, not once or twice, but three times. Peter blatantly denied knowing Jesus and even cursed to demonstrate the truthfulness of his lie.

Jesus pierced the wall of fear that caused Peter's denial with one look. Peter wept bitterly over his sin. I cannot imagine the agonizing guilt and self-hatred that may have plagued Peter's life in the three long days following his denial. He not only lost his Master, his Teacher, and his closest Friend, but he had denied that Friend in His darkest moment.

Perhaps this is why the angel took special care on that resurrection morning to ensure Peter got word of what had happened. The angel told Mary, *"Go your way, tell his disciples **and Peter** that he goeth before you into Galilee"* (Mark 16:7). The angel explained that Jesus was alive. Jesus wanted Peter to know. He also wanted Peter to know specifically that He planned to see him in Galilee.

What a message! The women returned to the disciples and told them that the Messiah had risen. The disciples were in disbelief. Luke says: *"Their words seemed to them as idle tales, and they believed them not."* Indeed, what a tale.

Peter had to see for himself; *"Then arose Peter, and ran unto the sepulchre..."* He was desperate for a ray of hope. After three days of agonizing guilt, he needed to ask the Master for forgiveness.

What a great example of forgiveness. Peter was forgiven of much. "Now, Peter, go and forgive others as I have forgiven you." Jesus had already taught him about forgiveness. I believe that Peter found it much easier to forgive after that resurrection morning.

Peter feasted on the great forgiveness he received, which enabled him to freely forgive others. This is the lesson from the parable, as the servant was forgiven of much, he should go and forgive others.

GIVE, GIVE, GIVE

Luke 6:38 is often quoted in sermons about tithes and offerings: *"Give and it shall be given unto you; good measure, pressed down, and shaken together, and running over, shall men give into your bosom. For with the same measure that ye mete withal it shall be measured to you again."*

Many people use that verse alone to teach that giving money to God (through tithes, offerings, and benevolence) will result in God rewarding you with financial blessings again.

The problem with this relaxed view of Scripture is twofold. Not only is Jesus *not* talking about money, but we are cheapening the meaning and value of what Jesus is really teaching by taking it out of context.

The sentiment of monetary giving and receiving may be found in other passages, but that is not the specific topic we find here.

If we temporarily ignored verse 38, there would be no doubt that Jesus is talking about forgiving others throughout the passage. He

FEASTING ON FORGIVENESS

says: *"be merciful...judge not...condemn not...forgive,"* which is basically saying similar points over and over again.

Then Jesus drops the verb *GIVE*.

Out of nowhere, does Jesus insert the topic of tithes and offerings? No. He is instructing those who follow Him to **give** forgiveness and mercy without condemnation to the same level or measure that we desire to be forgiven.

You are to be as merciful to others as God is merciful to you while judging, condemning, and then forgiving you. **Psalm 107:4** teaches that God's truth reaches to the clouds, but His mercy far surpasses that by reaching above the heavens. God wants to give us more forgiveness than we can handle.

> [35] But **love** ye your enemies,
> and do good, and lend, hoping for nothing again;
> and your reward shall be great,
> and ye shall be the children of the Highest:
> for he is kind unto the unthankful and to the evil.
>
> [36] Be ye therefore merciful,
> as your Father also is merciful.
>
> [37] **Judge not**, and ye shall not be judged:
> **condemn not**, and ye shall not be condemned:
> **forgive**, and ye shall be forgiven:
>
> [38] **Give**, and it shall be given unto you;
> good measure, pressed down, and shaken together,
> and running over, shall men give into your bosom.
> For with the same measure that ye mete
> withal it shall be measured to you again.
> **Luke 6:35-38**

HAPPY, HAPPY, HAPPY

You have opportunities with your enemies that you do not have with your friends. An enemy makes it possible for you to obey the law of Christ. Matthew 5:11 says: *"Blessed are ye, when men shall revile you, and persecute you, and shall say all manner of evil against you falsely, for my sake.* **Rejoice** *and be* **exceeding glad:** *for* **great is your reward** *in heaven: for so persecuted they the prophets which were before you."*

Forgiving others is an agreement that you have with God. It has nothing to do with their relationship to God. It has to do with your relationship with God and it is only possible because His loving nature is in you.

When Jesus told Peter to forgive seventy times seven, we know he was not giving a numerical threshold, but teaching always to forgive. How can we focus on *giving* forgiveness to those around us in a way that is pleasing to God?

Scripture says of the Lord when He forgave us, *"their sins and their iniquities will I remember no more."* (Hebrews 8:12). God did not forget what you did. He did not get selective amnesia, but rather He chooses not to remember. True forgiveness is not to *forgive and forget*. We may never forget what happened and neither does the Lord. ***True forgiveness is to remember that it has been forgiven.***

CHAPTER 13

FEASTING FOR STRENGTH

FEEDING THE HUNGRY SOUL

FEASTING FOR STRENGTH

You do not have to be an expert in biochemistry to know that food is fuel for the body. Every time you eat, your body converts your food into energy. If the body is well fed, you do not have to tell your organs to work; they just work. Likewise, if your spirit is properly fed, you do not have to tell your spiritual organs to work; they just work. Conversely, if your body or spirit is not properly fed, you do not have to tell them **not** to work; they will simply shut down all on their own.

In the same way that natural food is critical to the nourishment of your physical body; the fruit of the Spirit is critical to the nourishment of your spiritual body.

A lot of believers think victorious, abundant living is for someone else, but God wants all His children to experience the fullness and strength of the Holy Spirit.

The Apostle Paul was a man filled with the Holy Spirit. He said: "*I can do all things through Christ which strengtheneth me*" (Philippians 4:13)

Paul understood something; just like you need physical food for physical strength, you need spiritual food for spiritual strength. The fruit of the Spirit is our spiritual food. The Word of God is everything we need for spiritual sustenance.

Did you know it's possible to sit at a spiritual table and not eat? God's Word calls this type of person *carnal* because their appetites are not godly. These men and women are alive in Christ, but they are not *walking* in Him. It takes energy to walk. It is work. Believers must be careful to feed their spirit, which the scriptures refer to as the *inward* man.

FEEDING THE HUNGRY SOUL

> For which cause we faint not;
> but though our outward man perish,
> yet the inward man is renewed day by day.
> **2 Corinthians 4:16**

Just because you can quote scripture does not make you spiritual. Just because you can recite biblical truth does not make you spiritual. Memorizing scripture is not evidence of knowing the truth. You can memorize all the ingredients required to make homemade biscuits, but it's not the same as biting into one. When you are feasting on the fruit of the Spirit for the strength to walk in the Spirit, then you are a spiritual person.

Far too many believers are living in the flesh, not in the Spirit. You cannot deal with matters spiritually while being carnally minded.

If you are hungry and carnally minded yourself, how on earth can you deal sensitively and delicately with someone else who needs the Lord? You may teach them conformity, but you cannot adequately address the spiritual voids they are facing.

We will fall short every time we try to do something within our own power or our own will. Many people who have attempted to develop a relationship with God have been discouraged and even given up because they have tried to *earn* His acceptance rather than *receive* it.

Apparently, hypocrisy was a real problem in the early church. Throughout the book of James, the problem of self-deception regarding spirituality is addressed.

> [22] But be ye doers of the word, and not hearers only, deceiving your own selves.
>
> [23] For if any be a hearer of the word, and not a doer, he is like unto a man beholding his natural face in a glass:

FEASTING FOR STRENGTH

²⁴ For he beholdeth himself, and goeth his way,
and straightway forgetteth what manner of man he was.

²⁵ But whoso looketh into the perfect law of liberty,
and continueth therein, he being not a forgetful hearer,
but a doer of the work, this man shall be blessed in his deed.
James 1:22-25

God's Word is clear. We are saved by grace through faith, but we are also called to be doers and workers. James 2:26 says *"For as the body without the spirit is dead, so faith without works is dead also."*

Faith without works is dead because true faith transforms a life. It is also true that works without faith is dead. Jesus said that some would call Him "Lord," but would not enter the kingdom of heaven (Matthew 7:21-23).

There will be people at the Judgment who will not have demonstrated the fruit of good works. Others will have done works apart from faith in an effort to save themselves. All of our works are as filthy rags to God apart from Christ (Isaiah 64:6). They are tainted by our sin and not sufficient to transform us from being dead in our trespasses (Colossians 2:13) to being alive.

God wants us to be the kind of believer that Paul talks about; ones who are *"filled with the Spirit"* (Ephesians 5:18). No, Spirit-filled Christians are not exempt from falling, but they are yielded to God's Spirit. He works within them. Spirit-filled believers are fulfilled people with a "can do" attitude.

You have the seal of the Holy Spirit if you are a believer. The question is, are you indulging on the fruit? Are you allowing the Spirit of God to control your life, your days, and your destiny?

God has a work for you to do in your life. In 1 Corinthians 12, Scripture talks about our spiritual gifts. These gifts are great spiritual tools for accomplishing God's work, but they are useless unless we have been properly nourished with the fruit of the Spirit. So feast, because there's plenty of work to do.

CHAPTER 14

FEASTING WITH YOUR SOULMATE

Are we destined to have that one special "someone," the same way Adam had Eve?

Two people come together in holy matrimony. They may be of the same race and culture, with similar beliefs and expressions. They may be of the same race and creed. They may be deliriously happy and completely in love, but are they *soul mates*?

THE BIG LIE

The common idea of a *soul mate* is that for every person, there is another person who is a *perfect fit*. If you marry anyone other than this *soul mate*, you will never be happy. Is this concept of a *soul mate* biblical? No, it is not. It is one big cultural lie.

The concept of a soul mate is often used as an excuse for divorce. People who are unhappily married often claim that they failed to marry their soul mate; therefore, they should divorce and begin the search for their true soul mate. This is all wrong.

Feelings create illusions. After one of the terror attacks in Paris, a video made its rounds of a French father consoling his son with a strange illusion. The young boy feared the *mean men* with guns. Oddly, the father assured his son that the flowers and candles around the memorial were to fight against the guns used in the attack. The father had convinced his son fear was not necessary because of the flowers and candles. Of course these items did nothing to protect anyone, yet that feeling created the illusion of comfort for the young boy. Flowers may give us good feelings, but if we believe they serve as a defense against a lunatic killer, we will be deceived and unarmed.

The feelings of a *soul mate* may bring comfort and happiness for a time, but this illusion will always disappoint eventually.

WHAT IS LOVE?

Love is supernatural. Love is not something you give or receive. I used to believe that love was just a verb, but Scripture says otherwise. Love is a Being—God.

God is love. He does not need to conform to any standard for love; He is the standard. God's love can be like a window. It is so completely transparent, that we often fail to appreciate it. It is this transparency of God's love which enables us to see everything else we love. If we cannot see clearly, it is because our side of the window is dirty.

God is the very definition of love. Jesus taught us how to express this love. According to Christ, we are to express love toward the most undesirable of undesirables, even as God so loved the world (**John 3:16**). To love others properly; we must love others as Christ in all of His unattractive disguises (**Matthew 25:34-46**).

YOUR TRUE SOULMATE

Your Spouse is not your soul mate. A husband and wife are one flesh. They are not one spirit, and they are not one soul.

The Bible says that David was *a man after God's own heart*. What does that mean? Notice the wording in these psalms.

> [A Psalm of David.] Unto thee, O LORD, do I lift up my SOUL.
> **Psalm 25:1**

> As the hart panteth after the water brooks,
> so panteth my SOUL after thee, O God.
> **Psalms 42:1**

> My SOUL thirsteth for God, for the living God:
> when shall I come and appear before God?
> **Psalms 42:2**

As a husband, David loved his wife, but he loved God with all his soul.

As a father, David loved his children, but he loved God with all his soul.

As a king, David loved his Nation, but he loved God with all his soul.

You see, David was in pursuit of God's heart.

David's heart-compass was not horizontal, it was vertical. David understood that every relationship in the *flesh* is temporary. David longed for the eternal. The Spirit of God was David's soul mate.

If you're saved, you are betrothed. You are part of the future bride of Christ. He is your soul mate. His Spirit dwells with your spirit. He should be everything to you. He should be your all.

Why are people seeking their soul mate among flawed humanity? It is because our culture is empty. The soul of mankind is hungry and starving for true love—pure love. We long for that perfect love that will abolish every fear.

> There is no fear in love; but perfect love casteth out fear…
> **1 John 4:18**

LOVE OR LUST?

Proverbs 27:7 says, *"The full soul loatheth an honeycomb; but to the hungry soul every bitter thing is sweet."*

A malnourished soul will crave anything it can find, no matter how bitter. It will hunger continually. Even the bitter fruit of worldly love will appear sweet when the soul is hungry.

FEEDING THE HUNGRY SOUL

Your soul was created for love, not for the bitter fruit of the world. We were created to feast on True Love—God's love.

God is Spirit, and they that worship him must worship him in spirit and in truth. John 4:24

Married or unmarried, we all share the same soul mate—Jesus.

> Thou shalt love the Lord thy God
> with all thy heart,
> and with all thy SOUL,
> and with all thy strength,
> and with all thy mind;
> and thy neighbour as thyself.
> **Luke 10:27**

The hungry soul will equate lust with love, but these two could not be more opposed to one another. There is a great difference between the two, along with their outcomes. For example, David and Solomon were both great Kings in Israel. They both started out well; however, both committed grievous sin with women.

David had a lust problem. Solomon had a love problem. David's lust produced adultery. Solomon's many loves produced idolatry. Worldly lust will turn the head and worldly love will turn the heart.

Who is your soul mate? Who is your first love? This all depends on your relationship with God. Do you see Him as only the Law Giver or is He also your Love Giver?

People want to romanticize their lives. It's part of our culture, but after a while we all realize the emptiness in that narrative. We yearn for something deeper.

To love someone in Christ is to experience truth. Truth is scary. Truth has bad breath at times; truth can be boring; truth burns the food; truth isn't always pretty or handsome. Truth is rarely romantic. However, truth is strong. Truth is secure. Truth may fall, but it always rises. Truth is wild and untamed, yet safe.

Is God *your* soul mate?

Have you been spending enough time with your true Soul Mate? You should be feasting with Him every day.

CHAPTER 15

THERE IS ROOM

THERE IS ROOM

In Luke 14, Jesus describes the Kingdom of God as a great feast. Study this story and ask yourself these questions: *Whom in your life do you consider unworthy of your time?*

Whom in your life would you not invite to a cookout at your home?

Whom do you know that simply does not meet your standards, and would not be welcomed?

Simply put, is there anybody who is not worthy to come eat at your table?

What about God's table?

> And it came to pass, as he went into the house of one of the chief Pharisees to eat bread on the sabbath day, that they watched him.
>
> **Luke 14:1**

We see the extraordinary love of Jesus in going to eat at the home of those who were out to get him. They were looking for ways to discredit the Lord, yet he joined them for dinner.

A man with dropsy disease was standing outside the Pharisees' house. Dropsy is a condition of the heart and liver where the limbs and body are distended with water and remain terribly swollen. The Pharisees at dinner possibly hoped Jesus would heal the man on the Sabbath so they could accuse him of breaking the Jewish law. They knew his reputation for hanging around sinners. By the way, even in this area we should be like Jesus—spend enough time ministering to sinners that it ruins your reputation with religious people.

Jesus asked the Pharisees and experts of the law, "*Is it lawful to heal on the sabbath day?*" They remained silent. So Jesus "*took him, and healed him, and let him go*" (Luke 14:4). Jesus knew that the man would not be welcome in the home of the Pharisee.

FEEDING THE HUNGRY SOUL

The dining area of a chief Pharisee's home typically had three couches surrounding a huge table loaded with food in the center. A large couch was located at the head of the table farthest from the door with a smaller couch on each side of the table. Important people would be placed at the couches and others at places on the floor.

Jesus observed people elbowing for a place of honor near the head of the table. So, Jesus says: *"go and sit down in the lowest room; that when he that bade thee cometh, he may say unto thee, Friend, go up higher: then shalt thou have worship in the presence of them that sit at meat with thee"* (Luke 14:10). In other words, do not try to take the place of honor.

Then Jesus turned to his host and told him the next time he puts on a dinner, do not just invite friends, family, and rich neighbors—the kind of people who will return the favor. Invite some people who never get invited out. Invite the poor people from *the wrong side of the tracks.*

Our Lord made it clear to his host that ALL people should be invited to the table. The *moral majority* of Pharisees would never think of inviting the poor, crippled, lame or blind, but those are the people whom Jesus welcomes.

One of the men at the table heard what Jesus said and replied: "*Blessed is he that shall eat bread in the kingdom of God*" (Luke 14:15). This man understood what Jesus was teaching and he looked forward to being part of the feast in the Kingdom of God. He considered himself blessed because he knew he was welcomed at the table of Jesus in the Kingdom.

Jesus replied with a parable that we call "The Great Banquet." In this parable, a man planned a great dinner party and invited many people. When the time came, he sent out his servant to gather all his guests, saying: "Come on in; the food is on the table." However, when the servant approached the invited guests, one after another, they all made excuses for not going to the banquet.

One man said he bought a piece of property and he must go to see it. What a poor business man, buying real estate sight-unseen.

Another said he could not come because he bought a team of oxen, but he did not know if they were any good. What a lousy investor.

Yet another man said he could not come because he is married. This man was obviously a few bricks short of a full load because every married man knows how much women enjoy dressing up and going out to dinner. This guy might have found himself in hot water.

In any case, they were all invited guests and rudely snubbed their host.

As the Pharisees and guests listened to Jesus at dinner that night, they understood his message. Jesus was telling them that His Kingdom banquet was prepared and they all had invitations, but they each refused to come.

Outside the door stood the common people, the hookers, drunks, and all the undesirables. The next thing Jesus said in his story, "*Go out quickly into the streets and lanes of the city, and bring in hither the poor, and the maimed, and the halt, and the blind*" (**Luke 14:21**).

Jesus wants the misfits, homeless and wretched at his table. He wants to feast with them. He was including all those standing outside the door; those who find themselves neglected by the moral and religious elites. Everyone was being invited to sit at God's table. The invitation was to all people of all socio-economic standings, both rich and poor.

The servant in Christ's parable goes out and comes back and reports that he has done as he was told. Then in verse 22, we see the servant exclaim: *"and yet there is room."*

What a great promise. There is still room!

Then the Master said to his servant: "*Go out into the highways and hedges, and compel them to come in, that my house may be **FILLED**.*"

God loves to fill things up! He wants fullness, not emptiness. Leave no seat vacant.

LOVING SINNERS

The Pharisees hated sinners and they had deceived themselves into believing this was a good thing. There are a few scriptures in the Old Testament where King David and others speak of their hatred for the wicked. This hatred for the wicked was expressed under the inspiration of God in the scriptures. For example, Psalm 26:5 says: "*I have hated the congregation of evil doers; and will not sit with the wicked.*"

Does the psalmist's hatred for evildoers justify a believer doing the same?

Are believers supposed to hate sinners? Many believers feel they have the right to hate, hold grudges or despise certain people. They actually hate those who espouse abortion and *homosexuals*. If someone does them wrong, they feel vindicated when they hold feelings of ill will toward that person, or persons. Some believers go so far as to curse the wrongdoer.

How are we supposed to respond to sinners? Jesus Christ came to reveal God's covenant. Under the provisions of this covenant He gave believers a *commandment* regarding those who sin against God and are His enemies.

> 43 Ye have heard that it hath been said,
> Thou shalt love thy neighbour, and hate thine enemy.
>
> 44 But I say unto you, Love your enemies,
> bless them that curse you,
> do good to them that hate you,
> and pray for them which despitefully use you,
> and persecute you;
>
> 45 That ye may be the children of your Father
> which is in heaven:
> for he maketh his sun to rise
> on the evil and on the good,
> and sendeth rain on the just and on the unjust.
>
> 46 For if ye love them which love you,
> what reward have ye?
> do not even the publicans the same?
>
> 47 And if ye salute your brethren only,
> what do ye more than others?
> do not even the publicans so?
>
> 47 Be ye therefore perfect,
> even as your Father which is in heaven is perfect.
> **Matthew 5:43-48**

Notice the words of Jesus... "Ye have heard that *it hath been said*, 'Ye shall love your neighbor, and hate thine enemy.'" He did not say: "Ye have heard that it was *commanded by God*..."

False religion proponents will always modify the commandments of God to fit their own agenda just as Satan did in the garden with Eve. This includes allowing themselves the privilege of hating their enemies. Do not forget the teaching in the previous chapter about precepts, principles, and presumptions. Loving others (no matter if they are brethren or heathen) is a command. Which precept demands hatred of anyone? Is our hatred a precept or a presumption?

*We **should** hate sin.*

*We **should** hate the devil.*

*We **should** hate wickedness.*

*We **should** hate the rulers of the darkness in this world, which are devils.*

*We **should** hate every false way.*

For this reason, there *is* a time to hate. However, do not hate your human enemy—love him—it is a command.

Furthermore, you are commanded to love others even as Christ loves you. Think about that. Christ came to seek and to save those whom he knew would reject Him. He loved those who despised Him. He loved those who conspired against Him. He loved those who falsely accused Him. He even loved those who nailed Him to the cross. He laid down His life for all men because of his love. Therefore, as Christ loved you while you were yet a sinner, in like manner you should love others.

IF ANY MAN

Because of Christ's command to love others as He loves us, we are compelled to restore those who have fallen. We are called to invite them to the table with us.

> 1 Brethren, if a man be overtaken in a fault,
> ye which are spiritual, restore such an one in the spirit of
> meekness; considering thyself, lest thou also be tempted.
>
> 2 Bear ye one another's burdens, and so fulfill the law of Christ.
> Galatians 6:1-2

THERE IS ROOM

The scripture warns us to consider ourselves, lest we also be tempted. What does this mean? Will I be tempted to drink alcohol if I help restore a man addicted to alcohol? No, that is a general misunderstanding and not what this verse says at all. God's warning in this passage is to *spiritual* restorers who are operating in the *spirit of meekness*. They are exhorted to consider themselves, because they might very well be tempted to give up on the one needing restoration.

For this reason, those who restore must be walking in the Spirit. He or she must be spiritual. They must be feasting on the longsuffering, gentleness, and kindness of the Spirit. There is nothing more devastating to the life of one who has fallen than to be placed into the hands of one who professes Christ, but is not willing to restore in the spirit of meekness.

Many fallen believers have been permanently damaged because of men and women who were supposed to be restoring them, but refused to be filled with the Spirit. Unfortunately, churches are filled with spiritually dead people. Oh, they have spiritual vocabularies, spiritual wardrobes, spiritual hobbies and activities, and spiritual friends, but they are not spiritual people. They are moral. They are pretty. But they are not spiritual. Restoration cannot be done by anyone who is not spiritual. This is why God specifically commands that only the spiritual help restore.

Galatians 6:1 also has the stipulation "*If a man*." Many people like to narrow this down to any man they like, or any man they deem worthy, or any man who has not hurt them, or any man who has not caused them embarrassment, or—well, you get the idea. We like to classify who the man is, but God leaves it completely open to include any man.

Any man means your disgraced friend.

Any man means your enemy.

FEEDING THE HUNGRY SOUL

Any man means the one whose sins caused a mess in your church.

Any man is not some men, or sincere men, or men you like, or men you believe deserve it.

It is any man.

Jesus wants us to be open to all men, because all are welcome at His table. Who did Jesus use to seek you out? Did He use a loved one, a relative, a mother, a father, a friend or a neighbor? Are you seeking the lost? Are you inviting them to the feast?

They need to know—***there is still room.***

CHAPTER 16

GOD LOVES RESTORATION

GOD LOVES RESTORATION

Was David a fraud?

One of the most heartbreaking and confusing times is when a friend or loved one falls into sin. The scandal of an illicit affair or some other sexual escapade is most hurtful.

In 2 Samuel 11, God's Word tells of David's affair with Bathsheba and how he murdered his friend Uriah to cover it up. David's sin was egregious. He disgraced his name and tarnished his legacy.

It would be easy for someone in the moment to assume from David's behavior that his faith was fraudulent. However, was he a fraud?

One of the reasons Israel asked for a king in 1 Samuel, chapter 8 was to have someone lead them in battle. David's adultery took place in the spring when kings go off to war. David remained at Jerusalem while everyone else went off to fight. David was not where he should have been.

David was taking a rest while his soldiers were out fighting the Ammonites. As he walked around on his rooftop, he sees a beautiful woman named Bathsheba bathing in her home.

Poor Bathsheba has often been depicted as bathing on the roof in the open where she could be seen, but the text does not say that. David is on the roof, not her. She was likely unaware that anyone could see her. After all, the men were supposed to be at war. David walks on the roof; essentially the Old Testament version of browsing the internet alone at night. He points, he clicks, and then clicks again. He pauses; he zooms in on something that catches his eye. Then his feelings start to overpower him.

This is where sexual temptation begins for a lot of people. Their lives lack purpose and the allure of sex promises something. It is a distraction more than attraction that some people desperately crave. David began to believe a lie.

This is what happens in adultery and fornication. You begin to fill your void with lies. You deceive yourself. You begin to think of someone in terms of the pleasure they can provide for you and you forget you are dealing with a real person and real relationships. Notice how, in 2 Samuel 11:3, David's servant subtly tries reminding him that this is someone's daughter, someone's wife, someone's mother. Why is he doing that? It is because sin, especially sexual sin, almost always objectifies someone. You think of them only as an object of your pleasure and you forget that you are dealing with someone's life, and many times multiple lives.

Think about that for a moment. David was being remarkably selfish. He was tired, self-entitled, and bored. Sex had become a commodity instead of a covenant. Knowing all that we do about the details of David's salacious sin, I ask you, was he a fraud?

David was an adulterer.

David was a murderer.

David was a liar.

David was a thief.

David was a bad friend.

David was a fallen sinner.

But was David a fraud?

No, he was not! David was king. God appointed him king. David was king before his affair and David was king after his affair. David was called a man after God's own heart before his affair and still today is called the same. David's fall was horrific, not because he was a phony, but because he was not a phony.

GOD LOVES RESTORATION

David was a king who committed adultery, not an adulterer who became king. David was real. The adultery was fraudulent. The murder was fraudulent. The deception was fraudulent. Most of **what** David did during that dark period was fraudulent, but the **"who"** never changed. David was God's chosen.

God made David king. God knew that he would fall into sin with Bathsheba before David was ever born. Regardless, God still chose to make David king. David's kingship was not determined by his poor character, but by God's grace.

The next time you experience the hurt from a loved one's fall into sin, ask yourself this question: Is anyone loved by you because they deserve to be? Do you deserve God's love? Does anyone do anything for the Lord because of their own personal qualities, or is everything we do for Him based solely on His love and grace toward us?

DAVID'S RESTORATION

David did not work or earn his way back to God. David appealed to the mercy of God when, by faith, he trusted God's grace to accept him. He was confronted and he repented.

After David's restoration, he penned one of the most beautiful songs in Scripture. It is recognized all over the world, but I am afraid the familiarity has somewhat diminished our senses from seeing everything it has to say.

> [1] The Lord is my shepherd; I shall not want.
>
> [2] He maketh me to lie down in green pastures:
> he leadeth me beside the still waters.

> ³ He restoreth my soul:
> he leadeth me in the paths of righteousness
> for his name's sake.
>
> ⁴ Yea, though I walk
> through the valley of the shadow of death,
> I will fear no evil: for thou art with me;
> thy rod and thy staff they comfort me.
>
> ⁵ Thou preparest a table before me
> in the presence of mine enemies:
> thou anointest my head with oil;
> my cup runneth over.
>
> ⁶ Surely goodness and mercy shall follow me
> all the days of my life:
> and I will dwell in the house of the Lord for ever.
> Psalm 23

Notice David's phrase "*He restoreth my soul*" is actually a statement of conclusion. In other words, green pastures and still waters are the way God restores us.

The word "*restore*" means to replenish; to return to its original state. Restoring a soul means that God fills it up with Himself and returns the joy of life back to that individual. Notice it is not some general or physical restoration—"*He restoreth my soul.*"

Soul is a very important word in the Scriptures.

In Genesis 2:7, we read that God breathed into the bodily figure of Adam, "*and man became a living soul.*" Your soul is that central thing that is most *you about you*. Your body is to the soul as a glove is to a hand.

How Does God Restore a Soul?

GOD LOVES RESTORATION

David said: "*He maketh me to lie down in green pastures.*" King David is not saying that God forced him. Only demonic spirits force their way into the lives of people. God did not restore David against his will. God calls us first and woos us by the Holy Spirit. We respond and come to faith. Our move is always the secondary move, always a response to what God is already doing. In the same way that smelling food **makes** you want to eat, David is saying that God is making me want to rest in green pastures. The tender grass of those green pastures is where sheep are fed. It's the rich, lush feeding places from which the flock never needs to move in order to be satisfied. They can eat and sleep in green pastures.

Our *"green pastures"* is the bread of life and the fruit of the Spirit. God provides all the nourishment we need. We need it continually.

Next, the Lord led David beside the still waters. God essentially says of our own efforts, "What are you doing over there? Come over here. This is where the water is quiet. This is where you can be refreshed. My living water is deep and plentiful." This water will restore your soul. Sheep are scared of tumultuous water, and so are we. God provides the still waters by His thirst-quenching presence. He will totally satisfy your deepest longings every time you turn to Him (see John 7:37–38).

Notice the word "beside." This is not some down-to-the-river-and-out-again experience. You can live your life beside the still waters. It is not a monthly or a weekly thing; it is a day after day, continuous walk in the stillness of God's presence.

God invited David to a thanksgiving feast, a place where he could eat, rest, and enjoy God's goodness. After his devastating fall into sin, David came to a place in his life where he could say: "*The Lord is my shepherd; I shall not want.*" David was filled again with the Lord as his Shepherd. David had no wants—no more hunger. He was satisfied in the Lord.

God is still in the soul restoring business. He wants to restore souls. He loves restoration. Do you?

CHAPTER 17

THE FULLNESS *of* GOD

FEEDING THE HUNGRY SOUL

THE FULLNESS OF GOD

Ever since the fall of man in the Garden of Eden, God's universal plan has been to restore mankind to a place of communion wherein our hearts and lives are drawn back to Him. As we are positioned into a place of restored relationship with God, we find that our lives begin to once again demonstrate the authority over our environment and circumstances; in a similar manner to Adam's authority over his own surroundings in Eden.

> 14 For this cause I bow my knees
> unto the Father of our Lord Jesus Christ,
>
> 15 Of whom the whole family in heaven and earth is named.
>
> 16 That he would grant you,
> according to the riches of his glory,
> to be strengthened with might by his Spirit in the inner man;
>
> 17 That Christ may dwell in your hearts by faith;
> that ye, being rooted and grounded in love,
>
> 18 May be able to comprehend with all saints
> what is the breadth, and length, and depth, and height;
>
> 19 And to know the love of Christ,
> which passeth knowledge,
> that ye might be FILLED with all the FULNESS of GOD.
>
> 20 Now unto him that is able to do
> exceeding abundantly above all that we ask or think,
> according to the power that worketh in us,
>
> 21 Unto him be glory in the church
> by Christ Jesus throughout all ages,
> world without end. Amen.
> **Ephesians 3:14-21**

Paul was praying for his readers to be filled with God's Spirit so that they could comprehend more and more the immensity of God's love toward them in Christ.

FEEDING THE HUNGRY SOUL

God wants to fill you up.

In Genesis 1, God gave man the cultural mandate to take dominion over the earth and fill it. Over and over in Scripture we see God's desire to fill things.

> Can any hide himself in secret places
> that I shall not see him? saith the LORD.
> Do not I fill heaven and earth? saith the LORD.
> **Jeremiah 23:24**
>
> I saw also the Lord sitting upon a throne,
> high and lifted up, and his train filled the temple.
> **Isaiah 6:1**
>
> But will God indeed dwell on the earth?
> behold, the heaven and heaven of heavens cannot contain thee;
> how much less this house that I have builded?
> **1 Kings 8:27**

His desire now is to fill His children with the love of Christ. Paul is not praying that they would become believers; he affirms their salvation in Chapter one. We know they are believers because they had received the seal of the Holy Spirit already.

The question is whether they have a measure of Christ's presence that could be described as "full." Having the Spirit does not mean you are full of Him.

What about you? What occupies your life, time, and thoughts? God's will for your life is to be filled with His very presence. We should pray that God would fill us with Himself and destroy our every void.

If we feast in God's presence enjoying the fruit of the Holy Spirit, we will have the strength to endure everything that comes into our lives. We will know something that surpasses knowledge when Christ fills us up.

Being filled with the Spirit is not about spectacular miracles, but knowing the love of Christ in ways we never thought possible. When you know him as Lord, all other things are considered a loss to you. What things consume you? Are you satisfied? God's fullness is divine contentment.

GREAT GAIN

> But godliness with contentment is great gain.
> **1 Timothy 6:6**

The word "contentment" has suffered a great loss in our modern language. We have abused and ignorantly maligned the word. Nowadays, you might hear something like this: "Well, I guess you'll just have to be content with what you have." ***No, that's not right.*** Contentment is not some noble act of settling for less. *Contentment, scripturally speaking, is the state of ultimate satisfaction.* Contentment is that place of *no need*s and *no want*s.

In Paul's writing to the Philippian church, he urged them to not be anxious about anything (Philippians 4:6). He presented himself as an example of a man who had learned to be content in times of plenty and in seasons of external lack (Phil. 4:11-13).

How did Paul acquire this contentment?

Some people foolishly strive to annihilate their desires. Paul did not learn to desire *less* so that he could be content with less. In fact, Paul's dreams and desires were *heightened*, not *lessened*. Fulfillment to his desires did not come through worldly ambition or his own religious efforts. Paul had a fiery ambition that drove him to preach all over the Mediterranean, from Jerusalem to northern

Greece, until there was no place left for him to preach (Rom. 15:23). He was more active than the Energizer bunny on steroids!

Paul had learned to be fully satisfied on the goodness of God.

> My people shall be satisfied
> with my goodness, saith the LORD.
> **Jeremiah 31:14**

Paul knew the fullness of God.

Paul found everything he had ever wanted in the person of Christ – the source of his bliss and fulfillment. Those who indulge on the fruit of the Spirit lack nothing. This is the abundant life!

Intimacy with God should never become a striving work. Does anyone really believe that a person must remain in a state of dissatisfaction to be spiritual? Some people seem to believe that denying happiness is somehow pleasing to God. Unfortunately, the idea of *godliness with contentment* gets thrown out the window. In reality, it is the ungodliness that remains dissatisfied.

If you are tired of the performance-based, emotional rollercoaster of man-made religion, then get off that ride and start feasting. Trust in His finished work, not your own efforts. Rest in the knowledge that you are permanently plugged into Christ, whether you *feel* it or not. He is in control. Do not doubt just because you are not *feeling* it at the moment. It is not about a feeling; it is about being. The Scriptures do not exhort us to *feel* filled, but to **be** filled. Start feasting. Faith comes first, then the feeling.

As for me, I will behold thy face in righteousness: I shall be satisfied, when I awake, with thy likeness. (Psalm 17:15)

The fullness of God always means perfect contentment.

THE FULLNESS OF GOD

So what does a life that's filled with God's fullness look like? Are there any signs that someone is filled up with God? Yes! Look at **Ephesians 5:18-21**.

18 And be not drunk with wine, wherein is excess; but be filled with the Spirit;

19 Speaking to yourselves in psalms and hymns and spiritual songs, singing and making melody in your heart to the Lord;

20 Giving thanks always for all things unto God and the Father in the name of our Lord Jesus Christ;

21 Submitting yourselves one to another in the fear of God.

A person who is filled with God's fullness will have three distinguishing characteristics:

1) They will sing to the Lord and about the Lord (verse 19).

2) They will tell others about God's great love (verse 20).

3) They will gladly serve others because a life that is filled with the Spirit looks like the life of Jesus, Who laid down His life for His friends (verse 21).

Being intimately filled with God's Spirit assures every believer that the head of the serpent will be crushed and life will be lived as an *overcomer*.

What did God do so that I can be filled up with Him? God sent Jesus, who gave up everything, even His own life on the cross. The filling of the believer is possible only because Christ was emptied. He was utterly crushed and poured out on the cross so that we could be healed and filled with God's presence and love.

ON EARTH AS IT IS IN HEAVEN

Occasionally, certain words in the Scriptures jump out at me and almost take my breath away. Such was the case recently with the words "on earth as it is in heaven," in our Lord's Prayer. Jesus was teaching about our prayer for God's will to be done on earth as it is in heaven.

It is easy to generalize the idea of praying for everything on earth to function as everything does in heaven, but I recently saw it in a different light. I began to apply it specifically to my life, instead of using it as a broad general term. Suddenly, it came alive. Let me give you some examples that came to my mind.

Thy will be done…
…in my car as it is in heaven.
… in my home as it is in heaven.
… in my private life as it is in heaven.
… on my job as it is in heaven.
… in my relationships as it is in heaven.
… in front of my television as it is in heaven.
… on my computer as it is in heaven.

I could go on and on, but the point is that we generalize the term *on earth*. Most people probably do not apply it specifically in their daily life. Let's bring it down to the specifics of our lives. God has a will for everything we do. He has a will for how I behave in my car when another driver cuts me off. He has a will for me in the restaurant when I respond to a rude server. He has a will for every part of my life and I am to seek that will and obey it.

Unfortunately, most believers probably live a more generalized Christian life rather than a specific one. To do God's will on earth as it is in heaven is to do it specifically. It requires us to break down every component of our life and commit ourselves to do His will here as it is in heaven.

Perhaps we all need to specify more clearly what it is that we pray, so that we will become more conformed to the will He has for us on earth as it is in heaven.

STARVING THE IMAGINATION

A good actor will intentionally try to become the character they are portraying. Unfortunately, people are often guilty of trying to become the character they think others expect them to be. Unintentionally they write, produce and star in a role that is not meant for them. This is where depression often begins; you believe that you must be or do something according to this false narrative. This is one sure road that leads to depression.

Resting in Christ will release you for living this lifestyle of bondage and depression. Resting in Christ will release you from trying to live a scripted life that was not meant for you.

Sadness is not depression. Sadness is happenstance. Like happiness and the weather; sadness will pass. However, *depression* is your body saying, "I don't want to play this character anymore!"

We continually filter our thoughts; some we entertain and others we avoid. Some thoughts are real and some are not real. Even though you may have thought about leprechauns in the past, you know they are not real. You may have had thoughts about yourself in the past that are no different than a thought about leprechauns; they are not real. We must all be aware; Satan is a thief and he wants to manipulate your thoughts and steal your peace.

When you create a thought-idol with images, it is called **"imagination."** God's Word has nothing positive to say about imagination, not one thing. Please note that what we call *imagination* in our modern culture is not altogether the same meaning as the word for imagination used in Scripture. We often conflate dreams, visions, and imaginations, whereas Scripture makes a distinction. Dreams and visions are not the same as imaginations.

There are certain things that I dream of or envision doing one day, which are not imagined.

- A dream or vision always looks ahead. They concentrate on your future with true expectations. Imagination is a focus and manipulation of the past and present with false expectations. For example, I do not dream of one day becoming Abraham Lincoln, though some people may have imagined themselves to be him. I might dream of being like him, but only in the self-deception of imagination could one claim that they are or are becoming him.
- A dream or vision affects your life and the lives around you in the reality of God's world. Imaginations affect you and the lives around you in a world of your own making.
- A dream or vision is a parable of reality, while imagination is the abandonment of reality. Dreams and visions *reflect* what is true, while imaginations *deflect* what is true.
- A dream or vision feeds your spirit while imagination feeds itself like a parasite. For example, I am not against video games, but I believe that a good number of people become emotionally consumed by them. They abandon reality to hide in the imagination of the game.

"What about a child's imagination?" This is a defensive question that is incorrectly stated. The proper question should be "what

THE FULLNESS OF GOD

about the child's *ability* to imagine?" A child's ability to imagine is the same ability which God uses to give dreams and visions. The ability is good. A child will often pretend or play make-believe. This is an innocent way to exercise his ability to dream. However, the number of *adults* who live out their lives in make-believe is astounding and sad.

> When I was a child, I spoke as a child,
> I understood as a child, I thought as a child;
> but when I became a man, I put away childish things.
> **1 Corinthians 13:11**
>
> ³ For though we walk in the flesh,
> we do not war after the flesh:
>
> ⁴ (for the weapons of our warfare are not carnal,
> but mighty through God
> to the pulling down of strong holds;)
>
> ⁵ Casting down imaginations,
> and every high thing that exalteth itself
> against the knowledge of God,
> and bringing into captivity every thought
> to the obedience of Christ;
>
> ⁶ and having in a readiness to revenge all disobedience,
> when your obedience is fulfilled.
> **2 Corinthians 10:3-6**

Paul goes on to tell us in 2 Corinthians 10 that our strength is not in ourselves. Our fulfillment is not in ourselves. Our fulfillment is in Christ. In order to experience the fullness of God, we must starve our imagination and abide in Him.

Let us feast and be filled with God's presence. We need to know Christ's love more and more, living a life that's filled with love, and inviting everyone we meet to feast along with us.

Have you ever noticed what the scriptures say will happen to our bellies one day? Paul explains in 1 Corinthians 6:13, *"Meats for the belly, and the belly for meats: but God shall destroy both it and them..."* Our new bodies will not have an empty void. Everything we consume will be fully used by our bodies. Nothing will be wasted and no void will ever exist. It will be impossible to repeat Adam's transgression.

Furthermore, Paul adds in 1 Corinthians 15:28, *"And when all things shall be subdued unto him, then shall the Son also himself be subject unto him that put all things under him, that God may be all in all."* The fullness of God will be all in all. Every void will be completely and finally destroyed in Him.

CHAPTER 18

FEED MY LAMBS

FEED MY LAMBS

Jesus poured Himself out for us on the cross. God freely pours out His Spirit upon those who believe. Therefore, we are called to pour ourselves out before Him like a drink offering–spilling our hearts out on the dry ground of the earth–laying our lives down for our fellow man, as if in sacrifice to God Himself.

> Freely ye have received, freely give.
> **Matthew 10:8**

The world is full of hungry and thirsty people. They need help. They need to be fed.

Jesus was fairly explicit about this in the closing sentences of John's gospel. *"Feed my sheep, feed my sheep, feed my sheep."* Even if He had said it only once, we would have no wiggle room, but repeating Himself three times negates any excuses on our part. Jesus wants us to feed His sheep!

Jesus fed 5,000 men and gave His disciples the honor of helping. You know that feeding that many people is hard work, but they were excited to help. They were in ministry with Christ. They were yoked together with him. When you are yoked with Jesus, even hard work gives you rest! When the day was over and everyone had been fed, they gathered together twelve full baskets of food. The disciples who labored for Christ would now have a full basket for themselves. Our labor with Christ always comes with a reward.

Feeding sheep is costly. God's Word says: "*Buy the truth, and sell it not*" (Proverbs 23:23). Truth, especially proclaiming truth, will always cost you something, but a faithful servant will pour out his life for others. And a poured out life is like a sweet perfume to God.

Do you recall Mary Magdalene in John 12, pouring out her own expensive perfume—worth a year's wages—over the feet of Jesus as He sat at the table?

She anointed Him for the day of His burial. *"Then took Mary a pound of ointment of spikenard, very costly, and anointed the feet of Jesus, and wiped his feet with her hair: and the house was filled with the odour of the ointment"* (John 12:3)

This was one of the most dramatic demonstrations of worship in scripture. Yet Judas becomes incensed when that fragrance reaches his nostrils, arguing that the oil should have been sold and the money given to the poor. His thievery is exposed, and shortly afterward, he betrays the Lord altogether.

The pouring out of one's self to God in reckless abandoned faith provokes those around you either to blessing or cursing. Your outpouring will permeate the room. It is a catalyst. You will smell to them like Heaven's aloes or your garments will reek of hell's sulfur. There is no middle ground. The word of God always elicits a response and that response always hinges on the heart of the hearer.

The world is running over with selfish Pharisees who fleece the sheep and peddle nonsense for personal gain. Meanwhile, the flock starves to death on a diet with the spiritual equivalent of marshmallows.

Believers are supposed to have good news, not bad news. Why are we so bent on the negative? Stop telling people the bad things that are happening in your church. Stop telling people what is wrong with other people. You do not know who is already on the edge because of depression and your words of bad news just might push them over the edge. "Death and life are in the power of the tongue."

You cannot be filled with gossip and the Holy Spirit at the same time. The Holy Spirit would often tell us to pray for someone who needs our prayers if we were listening to Him instead of unholy gossip. We must be filled in order to be usable.

COUNSELING THE HUNGRY

Here is a list of questions that you might ask someone in counseling:

1. How is your relationship with God?
2. Do you consider yourself saved? If so, why?
3. What are your three greatest goals in life?
4. When did you last read the Bible?
5. When did you last pray?
6. How is your relationship with your spouse, parents, children, family, neighbors, and coworkers?
7. Do you enjoy your job?
8. Are you afraid of failure?
9. Do you consider yourself a hard worker?
10. Have you experienced recent changes at your job?
11. Do you exercise?
12. How well do you sleep?
13. Do you have any health problems?
14. Do you have a sex life?
15. Do you have problems paying your bills?
16. Do you have a monthly budget?
17. Do you and your spouse ever argue over money?
18. When did you last take a vacation?
19. Do you feel more organized or disorganized?
20. What was the last major change in your life?
21. Has anyone you love dearly died?
22. What is your greatest fear?
23. Do you feel like you have a problem with anger?
24. Have you ever been bitter toward anyone?

25. Do you feel depressed?

26. Is there anyone toward whom you feel resentment?

27. Do you feel guilty or ashamed about anything?

28. Have you ever discovered your purpose in life?

29. What do you feel are your greatest strength and weaknesses?

30. Does your life ever feel empty?

31. What are your top five TV shows?

32. Do you feel rested?

33. What does the word "hope" mean to you?

LISTENING AND HEARING

There is a remarkable difference between listening and hearing. The act of listening is not the same as hearing. Have you ever been to the dentist and left with your mouth numb? You can ingest the nastiest steak or the best steak in the world and never know the difference. You are ingesting it instead of tasting it.

The same is true of listening versus hearing. We often listen to people, but seldom hear them. Faith is not the product of listening to God's Word; faith comes by HEARING God's Word (Romans 10:17). Several times in the word of God we find these words: "To him that hath ears to hear, let him hear."

Hearing produces:

- Discernment
- Wisdom
- Revelation

These three produce what Scripture refers to as "understanding" or "knowledge."

When you listen without hearing you are vulnerable to confusion and contamination. You won't know the difference, like eating the steak with your mouth and taste buds numbed by drugs.

You are a *taker* when you *listen*, but you become a *giver* when you *hear*. Hearing means that you are giving your time, attention, thoughts, and a portion of your life to another person.

Always remember when counseling, a little pain exists behind every "I'm okay." So, do not just listen to the other person; hear them.

As a counselor, listen in order to hear. Determine if the individual's need is physical, spiritual, or both. For example, a man who is heavily addicted to meth certainly has a physical and a spiritual problem. Trying to resolve one while ignoring the other is an exercise in futility. A physical issue can often be a symptom of a spiritual problem. Therefore, a wise counselor will restore an individual by helping them find and fill the void. This may also help the physical symptoms that accompany the issue.

As Christian counselors, we must address spiritual problems with Scripture. It is our duty to help reach and restore others. It is our mission to help repurpose lives and see spiritual voids destroyed. If you believe that someone has a physical need that may require medication, refer them to a medical doctor. Do not attempt to artificially fill their void. There are some medical conditions that stem from the physical brain instead of the spiritual mind. It takes discerning wisdom and experience to understand the difference.

Some may struggle with certain chemical imbalances which require medical attention. In these situations, you must employ the wisdom and prudence to refer them to someone better suited to help that need.

FEEDING THE HUNGRY SOUL

Your Good Shepherd did not and does not fail to feed you as you look to HIM. He asks that you in turn labor with him and feed his lambs.

Your Good Shepherd never has left you hungry; let's not leave anyone else that way.

> "Feed my lambs."
>
> **—Jesus**

APPENDIX

The following material is a visual presentation of the core truths discussed in this book.

Artwork by:
Brandi Neighbors,
Eleven One Studios

Satan is a thief.

Satan is a murderer.

Satan is a destroyer.

He takes. He devours.

See **John 10:10; Malachi 3:11; Revelation 9:11**

Satan wants to take from you. He wants to steal from you. Satan is a void-maker. Can you think of some things that Satan has stolen or attempted to steal from you? **Name three.**

A spiritual void is not only an absence or emptiness. It is an emptiness that demands substance. It must be filled.

There are many words in Scripture which express or define voids:

Hunger, emptiness, lust, vanity, thirst, darkness, blindness, drought, dryness, tombs, and death, to name a few.

Perhaps the most prominent term for void is the word "evil." **Isaiah 45:6** — *the absence of God's peace creates evil. Evil is not a force.*

Choose three biblical terms that best describe your personal void.

Proverbs 13:12

"Hope deferred maketh the heart sick, but when the desire cometh, it is a tree of life."

Many people suffer heartache because Satan has stolen their hope.

Man's despair does not begin with the presence of some sin, but with the absence of something.

1. What is the difference between a hope and a wish?
2. Why do you believe the absence of hope is so deadly?
3. Notice the "tree of life" is not "sought after," but is imminently forthcoming. Thus, we are not supposed to work to obtain the tree of life, but to wait for it. Why do you believe Scripture places so much emphasis on waiting?
See **Psalm 37:9, Psalm 59:9, Isaiah 40:31**.

*A void is prime real estate for Satan. He wants to fortify every void with a spiritual stronghold. After reading **2 Cor. 10:3-4, Joshua 6,** and **Matthew 16:18**, what are some of the more obvious strongholds Satan has in our culture? Can they be destroyed?*

Ephesians 4:27 *"Neither give place to the devil."*

Satan takes up residence in the void. This is a foothold or stronghold. He is the prince of power of the air. The prince of nothingness. The Ruler of darkness, according to **Ephesians 6**.

183

Satan wants to fill your void. The problem is that he fills it with trash.

Some trash looks good—**John 8:44**

Satan is called Baalzebub which means "lord of flies." He gets this name because everything he offers is rotten as dung.

1) What does the Word of God call the body in **1 Corinthians 6:19-20**?

2) How is Satan described in **2 Corinthians 11:13-15**?

3) What happens when Jesus comes into the temple in **Matthew 21:12**?

See **Matthew 13:38-39**, **2 Corinthians 11:13-15** — Satan wants to corrupt your temple, but Jesus threw the moneychangers out.

Many people have filled their life's void with Satan's trash.

Proverbs 27:7

"The full soul loatheth the honeycomb; but to every hungry soul every bitter thing is sweet."

Hunger can drive a man to eat the inedible. Likewise, spiritual hunger drives a man to fill his void with poison.

Christians often attack the trash and ignore the void.

Read Luke 15:10-24

1) What was the dissident son willing to do in verse 16?

2) Before he *"came to himself,"* what did he do in verse 17?

3) How did the father respond in verse 23?

Problems with attacking the trash:

1) the trash becomes the issue, leaving the void unaddressed.

2) Morality becomes cherished more than spirituality.

3) the void only becomes more substantial.

Consider **Luke 6:1-5**. Satan's greatest accomplishment isn't the prostitute, it is the Pharisee.

1) What are some examples of "trash attacking" in society today?

2) What was the focus of the Pharisees in Luke 6:1-5?

3) Have you ever been guilty of focusing on the trash instead of the Lord?

Do you currently have a void in your life?

Ask yourself these four questions:

1) Am I currently struggling with a particular sin?

2) What kind of feelings do I have that seem to enable this sin?

3) Which element of the Spirit's fruit do I replace with that sin?

4) What do I want to be from this point forward—filled with trash or filled with the Spirit? We should be filled with the Spirit.

About the Author

Dr. David Johnny Nixon resides in Doerun, Georgia, where he serves as President of *Restoration Care Group*, a non-profit counseling ministry which serves local churches and families in America and around the world. He is the author of four books: *Christian Counsel for a Confused Culture*, *The Good Samaritan Pastor*, *The Perfect Gift*, and the highly acclaimed book, *Born That Way After All*.

Dr. Nixon is a Veteran of the United States Army and retired honorably from military service due to injuries sustained in the line of duty. He is also a member of two outstanding charitable organizations; Disabled American Veterans (D.A.V.), and the Wounded Warrior Project.

Dr. Nixon regularly receives invitations to speak for churches, schools, and seminaries in many different states and foreign Countries. He has been a pastoral counselor for a number of years and has been interviewed on a variety of television and radio programs. Pastor Nixon and his wife, Chrissy, have been married for 20 years and have five children—four girls and one boy. They enjoy life together as a family at their home nestled in the pines of South Georgia.

The *Restoration Counseling Center* offers Bible-based pastoral counsel with a specialty in helping those who are in conflict with their
sexual identity or their gender identity.

For more information or to seek help, visit us at:
www.Restoration.care

www.ingramcontent.com/pod-product-compliance
Lightning Source LLC
Chambersburg PA
CBHW060824050426
42453CB00008B/579